Great SHIPS
on the
Great LAKES

T0039648

Great SHIPS on the Great LAKES

A Maritime History

Catherine M. Green
Jefferson J. Gray
Bobbie Malone

WISCONSIN HISTORICAL SOCIETY PRESS

Published by the
Wisconsin Historical Society Press
Publishers since 1855

Publication of this book was made possible in part by a generous grant from Thunder Bay National Marine Sanctuary and the Michigan Historical Center.

wisconsinhistory.org

Front cover: The schooner *John J. Audubon* lies 170 feet deep in Lake Huron. Photo by Doug Kesling, NOAA, Thunder Bay National Marine Sanctuary

Back cover images: Photo of diver investigating the *McCool* off the coast of Bayfield, Wisconsin, by Tamara Thomsen, Wisconsin Historical Society; Photo of Thunder Bay Lighthouse, Thunder Bay Sanctuary Research Collection

Frontispiece: The *City of Alpena* steamer, courtesy of the Thunder Bay Sanctuary Research Collection

Printed in the United States of America

Designed by Composure Graphics

14 13 12 11 10   1 2 3 4 5

Library of Congress Cataloging-in-Publication Data
Green, Catherine, 1974–
  Great ships on the Great Lakes : a maritime history / Cathy Green, Jefferson J. Gray, Bobbie Malone.—1st ed.
      p. cm.
  Includes index.
    ISBN 978-0-87020-582-8 (pbk. : alk. paper) 1. Ships—Great Lakes (North America)—History—Juvenile literature. 2. Shipping—Great Lakes (North America)—History—Juvenile literature. 3. Navigation—Great Lakes (North America)—History—Juvenile literature. 4. Great Lakes Region (North America)—Navigation—History—Juvenile literature. I. Gray, Jefferson J. II. Malone, Bobbie, 1944- III. Title.
  VK23.7.G724 2013
  386.0977—dc23
                                              2013008043

∞ The paper used in this publication meets the minimum requirements of the American National Standard for Information Sciences—Permanence of Paper for Printed Library Materials, ANSI Z39.48-1992.

Contents

1 What Is Maritime History? 1

2 Lakes, Rivers, and Ice 2

People Tell Stories about Great Floods 6

The Great Lakes under Water 7

The Great Lakes under Ice 8

Melting Glaciers Create Lakes 9

Great Lakes Shorelines 10

Wetlands 12

Rivers and Their Watersheds 14

3 Paddles and Pelts 16

Native People of the Great Lakes 16

Dugout Canoes 18

Birchbark Canoes 19

Europeans Travel the Great Lakes 21

The Canoes of the French Fur Traders 23

The Mysterious Disappearance of the *Griffon* 26

Exploration, Not Settlement 28

4 Fighting for the Inland Seas 30

Europeans Build Forts 30

The French and Indian War 33

How Did the Revolutionary War Affect the Great Lakes? 34

Pioneering Spirit 36

Battle on the Lakes: The War of 1812 36

African American Sailors 40

Why Were Sailing Ships Important to the War of 1812? 40

5 Connecting with Canals **44**

The Push West 45

The Erie Canal 46

The Great Lakes and the Great Eight 48

Building along the Great Lakes Waterways 50

6 Sail and Steam **53**

Early Shipping 55

The Great Lakes Schooner 55

How Locks Work 58

Steam Engines 60

Bigger and Faster Ships 62

Great Lakes Shipping Today 67

7 Sailors and Keepers **70**

The Sailor's Life 71

Lighthouses 74

Lighthouse Keepers 78

Lighthouse Families 80

8 Shipwrecks **84**

The "Shipwreck Century" 85

Shipwreck Alley 86

Thunder in Thunder Bay: The *Isaac M. Scott* 88

Shallows and Shoals: The *New Orleans* 90

Crowded Shipping Lanes: The *Pewabic* 92

Fire! The *Montana* 95

The Death's Door Passage 96

"Captain Santa" and the Christmas Tree Ship 98

A Superior Shipwreck: The Sinking of the *Lucerne* 101

9 Exploring Shipwrecks **104**

Shipwrecks, Shipwrecks Everywhere 105

The Sinking of the *Cornelia B. Windiate* 106

Searching for Shipwrecks 108

Documenting Shipwrecks 111

Conserving Shipwrecks 115

What is a National Marine Sanctuary? 117

Past, Present, and Future 119

Time Line **120**

To Learn More **124**

Places to Visit **127**

About the Authors **129**

Index **131**

What Is Maritime History?

When we study history, we use stories and clues from the past to help us understand events and why they happened. If we get our stories and clues from the lakes, seas, or oceans, then we are studying **maritime** history. This is a maritime history book. It uses stories and clues from the Great Lakes to explain how people in the Great Lakes region used their **natural resources**, including the lakes, to live their lives. And it tells about the many different types of boats people built to help them follow their dreams.

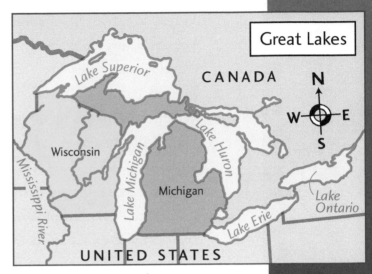

University of Wisconsin Cartography Laboratory

For thousands of years, people have used lakes and rivers in the Great Lakes **region** to travel and move their **goods**. In the time before there were streets, railroads, and highways, water was the best way to move people and the things they used or wanted. Why was traveling by water easier than traveling by land? How did people use waterways for transportation? Where did people go? What kinds of boats did they use? How did those who came from other places reach the Great Lakes region? These are some of the questions this book will answer.

---

maritime (mer uh tɪm): having to do with lakes, seas, or oceans
natural resources: resources that are found in nature, such as fresh water, minerals, and wildlife
region (ree juhn): area
goods: things that someone owns or things that are sold

Lakes, Rivers, and Ice

Water. We drink it. We wash dishes, take baths, fish, and swim in it. We canoe, water ski, sail, and ice skate on it. We also **ship** things and travel across water. We even make power from water. Water is part of everything we do and is absolutely necessary for all life on earth. Water even makes up 60 percent of our own bodies!

Luckily, the Great Lakes region has plenty of water. With Lakes Superior, Michigan, Huron, Ontario, and Erie, much of the northern border of the region is formed by water. And water is everywhere in between—with thousands of lakes and thousands of miles of rivers and streams. In fact, the states of Minnesota, Wisconsin, and Michigan and parts of Indiana, Ohio, Pennsylvania, New York, and the Canadian **province** of Ontario have so many lakes and rivers that much of the land is actually *under* water! No matter which direction we travel, we can find a waterway, a body of water deep and wide enough for people to **navigate** a boat.

Smaller waterways, such as creeks or ponds, may only be large enough for a small boat, like a canoe. The Great Lakes, however, are large enough to allow huge ships to travel them. For thousands of years, people have used large and small waterways to travel and to move their goods. **Transporting** goods led to business and trading with folks living in areas that border these waterways and those who lived beyond. People have also used these waterways to supply other

---

ship: to send things by water
province: state
navigate: successfully steer
transporting: moving something from one place to another

needed natural resources, such as fish and plants. More recently people have enjoyed vacations on our lakes and rivers. By learning about waterways in the Great Lakes region and how people have used them, we can learn a lot about the ways people have lived and worked here.

A **freighter** in Green Bay Harbor, Wisconsin, about 1990
Wisconsin Department of Tourism

Two people **kayak** on the Detroit River.
Michigan Sea Grant

---

freighter (**fray** tur): a large ship
kayak (**kɪ** ak): paddle a slim, light boat with pointed ends

How did so much water find its way into our region? How has it shaped our landscape? In this chapter we will explore the answers to these questions, but we will find ourselves asking many more as we navigate our way through this book.

Although we may not often think about the water around us, it has amazing qualities. It's like a superhero! It can easily and quickly change from steam (gas) to water (liquid) to ice (solid). Water is strong like a superhero, too. By pushing up against or supporting floating objects, water can lift and move heavy materials—from huge logs to ships made of steel and concrete. And just like a superhero, water can change its shape. Water always moves to the lowest point and takes the shape of whatever it fills—a bowl or a glass, or a lake or a riverbed.

Steam (Gas)   **Water (Liquid)**   **Ice (Solid)**

Illustration by Jill Bremigan

No matter what form it takes, water can be very forceful. That is why floods are one of the most powerful natural disasters. For example, a river can flood when winter snow melts too quickly or when rainfall is very heavy. During a flood, the river spills over its banks. The water from the flood can cover an area in a short time. Sometimes a flooding river contains enough power to destroy buildings or change the way an entire landscape looks.

Even small amounts of water, moving over a long period of time, can wear down huge rocks to form caves and cliffs. This is what happened in the Pictured Rocks National Lakeshore along the shoreline of Michigan's Upper **Peninsula** and in the caves on Bayfield Peninsula along Lake Superior. Both the fast and slow movements of water and ice have completely shaped the Great Lakes and changed the land and waterways surrounding them. Movements of water and ice helped the Great Lakes region look as it does today.

Wisconsin's Bayfield caves were formed by water wearing down huge rocks over a long period of time.
Tamara Thomsen, Wisconsin Historical Society

Pictured Rocks National Lakeshore is located along the shoreline of Michigan's Upper Peninsula.
Dean Ducas

peninsula (puh **nin** su luh): an area of land that sticks out into the water

People Tell Stories about Great Floods

Water's terrific power has always amazed people. Many groups around the world have passed down stories that tell of great floods that completely changed the Earth. If you are Christian or Jewish, you may know a story about a great flood that includes animals marching into an ark two by two and a dove carrying an olive branch to show that land was beginning to appear again.

In *The Mishomis Book*, **Ojibwe** author Edward Benton Banai shares his people's story of a great flood. Here is a short version of that story:

Illustration by Joe Liles

At one time, people on Earth had lived in harmony. Then they began to lose respect for one another and fight. The Creator, **Gitchie Manito** decided to free the people of evil by sending a flood of water to cover the Earth. The flood came so fast that the Earth's living creatures were not prepared. Most drowned, but some were able to swim and search for land.

Original Man, or **Waynaboozoo**, and some animals climbed on a huge floating log. Waynaboozoo and many of the animals dove down into the water, but none could dive deep enough to find land. Finally, it was Muskrat who reached the bottom, but he could not hold his breath long enough to make it back up. He drowned on his return to the surface, but he managed to save a bit of earth in his paw. Turtle felt that this bit of soil could create a new Earth, so he asked Waynaboozoo to put it on his back. As the wind began to blow, the earth on Turtle's back began to grow until it became an island in the water. Here life could begin once more, and all creatures could live in peace. Today many Native people still give special honor to the turtle for bearing the weight of the new Earth on its back.

Ojibwe: oh **jib** wuh
Gitchie Manito: **git** chee **man** i toh
Waynaboozoo: way nuh **boo** zhoo

The Great Lakes under Water

Geologists are scientists who study rocks to find clues that reveal Earth's history. Some clues have helped geologists learn about the way water transformed the area that became the Great Lakes region. They have found that long ago our entire region was covered by a shallow sea filled with **marine** life. Over a long period of time, shells and coral collected on the sea floor and slowly hardened into huge layers of rock known as limestone. You can still see limestone along cliffs, in caves, or in **quarries**. Limestone reminds us that the entire region was once at the bottom of a sea.

A limestone quarry in Rogers City, Michigan.
Photograph by Matt Bower

geologists: jee **ol** oh jistz
marine (muh **reen**): related to water
quarries (**kwor** eez): places where rock has been blasted or cut away

The Great Lakes under Ice

Until about a million years ago, the Earth was much warmer than it is today. Then the climate grew colder. To the north of the Great Lakes, more snow fell in the long winters than could melt during the short summers. As the snow piled deeper and deeper, the lower layers turned into giant sheets of ice called **glaciers**. The climate stayed cool and the glaciers grew larger—more than a mile thick in some places!

Over thousands of years, the weather changed back and forth, from colder to warmer and warmer to colder. The colder periods are known as ice ages. During the ice ages, the edge of one of these sheets of ice moved very slowly, like cold, thick syrup, toward the Great Lakes region. The flowing ice was so heavy that it carved deep scars into the ground. As ice scraped down the landscape, it picked up and moved huge amounts of clay, sand, pebbles, and larger rocks. This combination is known as drift. A glacier acted like a bulldozer, pushing the drift to its outer edge.

Scientists think as many as eight to twelve ice ages occurred. Each lasted around 50,000 years. The last ice age ended around 14,000 years ago. That's when the last glacier began melting as the Earth warmed back up. The edges of the glaciers melted back when temperatures grew warmer. Advancing glaciers had already scraped off the highest places on the landscape, such as mountaintops. As the ice melted, the drift was dumped on the land and filled in the lowest spots. This process created the gently rolling landscape that you can see today in most of the **glaciated** areas in the Great Lakes region.

---

glaciers: glay shurz
glaciated (glay shee ay thud): once covered by glaciers

A modern-day glacier in Alaska
U.S. Geological Survey / Photograph by
Bruce F. Molnia

Melting Glaciers Create Lakes

Glaciers also created the Great Lakes. The enormous weight of the slowly moving glaciers deepened large **basins** of land in the area where we now find the lakes. These very deep basins filled with fresh water when the ice that made up the glaciers melted. The sand, gravel, and boulders picked up and carried by the glaciers were also left behind as the glaciers melted. These materials helped trap the water and form a landscape where people could live, as they've done for thousands of years since.

Together, the five Great Lakes stretch across about one thousand miles of the United States and Canada. They contain 20 percent or one-fifth of Earth's drinkable water. That's 65 trillion gallons! The Great Lakes serve as one of the most important waterways in the world.

---

basins: low areas

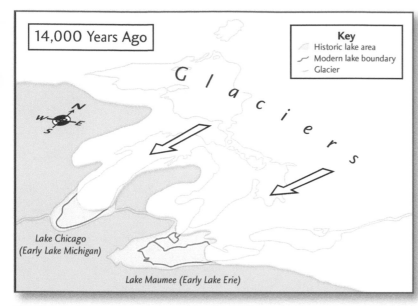

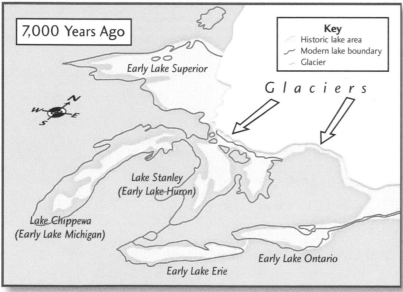

Glaciers from what is now Canada created the Great Lakes.
University of Wisconsin Cartography Laboratory

Great Lakes Shorelines

Have you ever wondered what gave the Great Lakes their **unique** shapes? As the glaciers moved slowly toward the south, they met some **obstacles**. The glaciers had to move around steep, rocky areas like Wisconsin's Door County Peninsula in Lake Michigan. Door County Peninsula gives Wisconsin the "thumb" of its mitten shape. Bruce Peninsula on Lake Huron's Canadian shore has "flowerpot" rock formations. So does Pictured Rocks National Lakeshore on Lake Superior in Michigan. Both of these peninsulas are examples of some

unique (yoo **neek**): the only one of its kind
obstacles (**ahb** stuh kuhlz): things that block a path

of the rocky ridges that blocked the paths of the glaciers as they slowly flowed across the land.

Cliffs and rocky peninsulas are only one kind of shore formed by **retreating** glaciers. The Great Lakes have over 8,300 miles of shoreline in the United States alone. The miles of shoreline can look very different because of the many varieties of soil and rocks in the region. The shore can be rocky like Pictured Rocks National Lakeshore or the Apostle Islands National Lakeshore along the southern shore of Lake Superior, sandy like Sleeping Bear Dunes National Lakeshore on the eastern shore of Lake Michigan, or have **wetlands** like Point **Pelee** National Park along the northern shore of Lake Erie. All of these special areas are part of US national park systems. But a coastline doesn't have to be a national park to be special. If there is a shoreline near you, what is it like? What other kinds of different Great Lakes shores have you visited?

Great Lakes Waterways by the Numbers							
	Michigan	**Wisconsin**	**Ohio**	**Illinois**	**Indiana**	**Minnesota**	**Pennsylvania**	**New York**
Miles of Great Lakes Shoreline	3,288	860	262	63	50	189	51	577
Number of Lakes	Over 11,000	14,949	Over 2,500	Over 3,000	No data	11,842	No data	7,849
Miles of Rivers and Streams	36,000	44,000	44,000	87,110	35,000	69,200	No data	52,337

retreating: moving back or away from a place
wetlands: areas covered with water for all or part of the year
Pelee: **pee** lee

Stairway to the Sea

Four of the five Great Lakes are at different **elevations**. A lake's elevation is how high it is above **sea level**. These lakes form a kind of staircase in the landscape for water to flow along, all the way down to the Atlantic Ocean. All five individual lakes are connected to each other through rivers and **canals**. These rivers and canals help form one giant lake system.

Each day, water flows from the **headwaters** of Lake Superior down through the connecting waterways of this lake system to Lake Erie. From Lake Erie, water eventually finds its way out to the Atlantic Ocean. That water has to follow a drop of more than six hundred feet to reach sea level at the Atlantic Ocean. About 326 feet of that drop occurs at Niagara Falls alone! Even though much water flows out of the Great Lakes and into the Atlantic Ocean, it is actually less than 1 percent of the total amount of water in the Great Lakes in any year.

Niagara Falls, where water from the Great Lakes travels on its way to the Atlantic Ocean
Wikimedia Commons

Wetlands

The Great Lakes' waterways also provide important habitats, places where fish and **aquatic** plants live beneath the surface of the water. When the glaciers melted, they created many of the freshwater lakes we have now. Some of these lakes were so shallow that aquatic plants slowly filled them in. We call these areas wetlands because they are covered with water for all or part of the year. Swamps, marshes, and bogs are examples of wetlands.

Wetlands are open areas without many trees. Yet wetlands are filled with many grasses, reeds, and other plants. The thick plant

---

elevations: levels above or below the ocean
sea level: the surface level of the ocean
canals (kuh **nalz**): waterways made by people
headwaters: source
aquatic (uh **kwa** tic): living in water

life in wetlands also serves as a welcoming habitat for many wild creatures. The water level in wetlands changes with the seasons or the amount of rainfall.

For many years, people thought wetlands were not valuable. They were full of mosquitoes. They were difficult to travel through or around. And they were hard to farm and difficult to build anything on. People filled in wetlands with dirt or built channels to drain the water from them.

The Alpena wetlands in Michigan are covered with water all or part of the year. They're filled with grasses, weeds, and other plants.
NOAA, Thunder Bay National Marine Sanctuary

Today, two-thirds of the wetlands that were once in the Great Lakes are gone. You can probably find places in your area where wetlands have been destroyed. But wetlands are very important to keep around, and not just because they provide habitats for plants and animals. Wetlands act like sponges. They keep harmful things from getting into waterways. Wetlands soak up things like **pollutants**, washed-away soil, and floodwater. Now most people understand that wetlands are an important part of Great Lakes **ecosystem**. Many groups, like the Wisconsin Wetlands Association and Michigan Wetland Restoration and **Watershed** Planning are working to **restore** wetlands.

---

pollutants: man-made substances that spoil natural resources
ecosystem: all the living things in a place and their relation to the environment
watershed: the region or land area that drains into a river or lake
restore: bring back to the original condition

Rivers and Their Watersheds

You've learned about water's amazing ability to transform the land around it. Water drains from the land into the nearest wetland and waterway—whether it's a pond, lake, stream, or river. The areas of land that drain into the same waterway form a watershed.

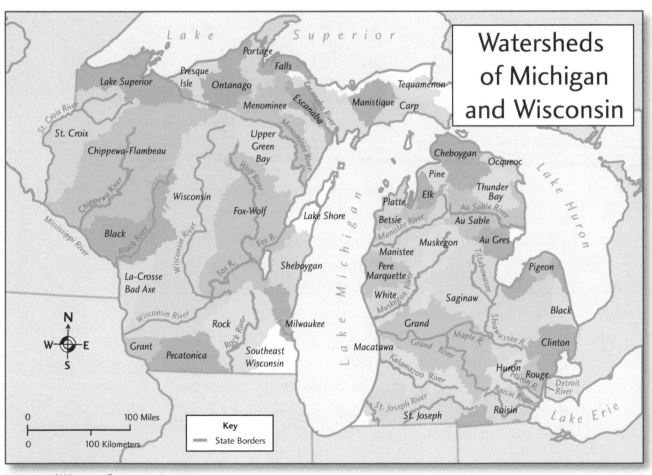

University of Wisconsin Cartography Laboratory

When a small stream flows into a larger waterway (such as a river), the stream is called a **tributary**. The tributary increases the river's size.

Large rivers and their tributaries form river systems. The river systems in the Great Lakes region are what allow water to move between the lakes and eventually flow all the way down to the Atlantic Ocean. In the next chapter, you'll learn more about how our different waterways served as our earliest highways.

---

tributary: trib yoo tair ree

3

Paddles and Pelts

Can you imagine your city or town without streets, roads, highways, railroad tracks, bike trails, or sidewalks? People have built many kinds of paths across our communities, states, and country. These transportation routes remind us that most of the time we travel *across land* to school, soccer practice, stores, or the homes of friends or family. Because we travel on land so much today, we often see water as an obstacle to go around or get across. But water really was and is helpful to transportation. In fact, for thousands of years water was the best way to move people and the things they needed or wanted.

Native people traveled all over the Great Lakes region without railroads, marked streets, or paved highways. The only "roads" were narrow paths that people traveled on by foot. People living here used waterways as the best and fastest way to get around. Explorers, fur traders, and others who came to the region later on also found that waterways were the best transportation routes.

Why was traveling by water easier than traveling by land? How did people use waterways for transportation? Where did people go? What kinds of boats did they use? How did those who came from other places reach cities in the Great Lakes region, such as Duluth, Chicago, Milwaukee, Detroit, and Buffalo? These are the questions this chapter answers.

Native People of the Great Lakes

Native people have lived in the Great Lakes region for thousands of years. They made their homes near streams, lakes, and rivers.

Waterways and wetlands served as key places to fish, hunt, and gather plants. Canoes helped Native people reach natural resources in places that their feet could not take them. Canoes helped people travel easily and carry large amounts of food and other supplies. Canoes were useful for spearing fish and gathering wild rice. And fish and wild rice were two important sources of food for many groups in the area.

Indians in the Great Lakes region made much of what they needed from nearby natural resources. But they also depended upon other materials that came from farther away. Native people traveled on the region's many waterways to trade their goods with each other. It was sometimes easier to trade with someone three hundred miles away by water than with someone thirty miles away across land! People living in the Great Lakes region used two basic kinds of canoes—dugout and birchbark—to gather food and supplies and to transport them from one place to another. Of course, families could also visit with relatives who lived elsewhere by traveling over water to reach them.

Three Indian women harvesting wild rice, about 150 years ago
WHi Image ID 9023

The Lake Mary Canoe

In the summer of 1996, a young girl went boating with her grandfather on Lake Mary in Kenosha County, Wisconsin. As they pulled up to the dock, she saw a strange piece of wood sticking out of the mud. From its smooth surface and a pointed end, they thought that it might be part of a canoe. They left the wood in the water, but talked to **underwater archaeologists** about what they found. Underwater archaeologists from the Wisconsin Historical Society went to investigate the wood. They found that it belonged to a dugout canoe made nearly two thousand years ago—one of the oldest boats found anywhere in the Great Lakes region.

Indians make a dugout canoe in this print from the 1700s.
Courtesy of the John Carter Brown Library at Brown University

Dugout Canoes

People carved or hollowed out a dugout canoe from the trunk of a large tree. Dugout canoes were heavy. But they worked well on slow-moving, shallow rivers, in lakes, and in marshes. People used dugouts for thousands of years, and children learned from their elders how to build them. **Techniques** for constructing dugout canoes changed very little over time.

If you tried to make a dugout canoe today without power tools, you might use the same techniques that Native people throughout the Americas used. First, they selected and cut down a tree with a straight trunk, long enough and wide enough to hollow out. Second, canoe makers stripped off the branches and scraped off the bark. Third, they hollowed out the log so the canoe would have a place for them to sit and store their goods.

---

underwater archaeologists (arh kee **ol** uh jists): scientists who explore and study shipwrecks and other underwater sites
techniques (tek **neeks**): ways of doing things that require certain skills

To hollow out the log, Native people used fire. The burned wood was easier to chip out. To control the fire canoe makers packed wet mud around the areas of the log they did not want to burn. They repeated these steps until the dugout was the right shape and thickness.

An Ojibwe man shapes birchbark in a frame to make a canoe, 1927.
WHi Image ID 41466

Birchbark Canoes

Native people made another type of canoe from the bark of birch trees. Birchbark canoes had many **advantages** over dugout canoes. First, birchbark canoes were much faster than dugouts. Birchbark canoes were also light enough to **portage**, or carry around shallow areas or waterfalls where it was difficult or impossible to navigate in the water. These canoes were strong enough to navigate through **rapids**, yet would not easily **capsize** in deep water. Although they were more fragile than dugouts, birchbark canoes were easy to repair. And there were plenty of birch trees around for materials. Birchbark canoes could also carry more goods and people, and they worked well for either lake or river travel.

A group of French traders making a **portage,** around 1879
WHi Image ID 7009

advantages: things that help you or put you ahead
portage (**port** idj): a place where canoes had to be carried, or to carry around a portage
rapids: parts of the river where the water runs very fast, usually over rocks
capsize: tip or turn over

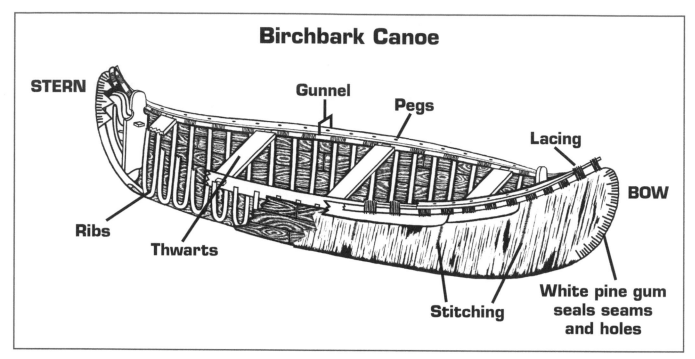

Birchbark Canoe

STERN

Gunnel

Pegs

Lacing

BOW

Ribs

Thwarts

Stitching

White pine gum seals seams and holes

After shaping the canoe, men cut the gunnels the right length and used steam to bend the ribs. Women sewed the birchbark pieces together. After stitching these to the boat, they sealed it using **pitch** from a white pine.

Illustration by Jill Bremigan

Men and women worked together to build birchbark canoes. Men chose a birch tree of the size they wanted. But they did not **fell** the tree. Instead, they cut and carefully removed long strips of bark from the tree. They used the bark strips to construct the body of the canoe. Besides the bark, canoe builders needed wood to make the boat's frame. Women gathered and used pine pitch for sealing. The basic canoe shape that Native people created is still used today, even for canoes made of modern materials like fiberglass or aluminum.

pitch: a sticky substance made from pine tree wood
fell: cut down

Europeans Travel the Great Lakes

When European explorers and fur traders began arriving in North America in the early 1600s, they had no maps to guide them. They wanted to get to what were known as the East Indies. The Europeans were looking for spices and valuable metals like gold and silver. They had no idea how large the North American continent was. At first, they hoped to find a waterway that was a shortcut across North America. But the explorers were disappointed to find that no such waterway existed.

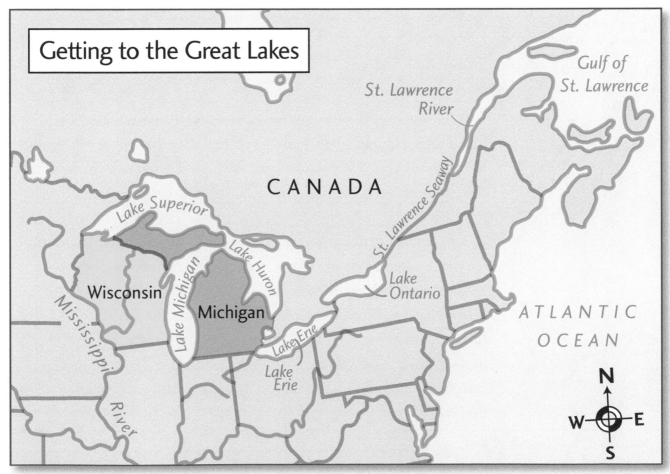

Early European explorers and settlers traveled to the Great Lakes using the St. Lawrence Seaway.
University of Wisconsin Cartography Laboratory

A French explorer named **Jean Nicolet** was the first European to see Wisconsin. For many years, he lived among the Indians in what is now Quebec, Canada.
WHi Image ID 1870

However, they did find many waterways that **penetrated** a land full of valuable plants and animals. Explorers used the Great Lakes and their connecting waterways to gather these natural resources. Then the explorers took them in their ships back across the Atlantic Ocean to Europe.

This time of exploration was also a time of **exchange**. Europeans had never seen anything like Native birchbark canoes. They were amazed that the canoes were so easy to navigate and portage. Europeans used the birchbark canoes to cross the Great Lakes and travel up and down the rivers in search of goods, such as animal **pelts**. Native people also enjoyed the trade. They began to use European-made goods, including iron pots, rifles, and wool cloth to make their lives easier.

Jean Nicolet: zhon nik oh **lay**
penetrated: went deep into
exchange: giving something in return for something else; trade
pelts: animal skins with fur

The Canoes of the French Fur Traders

The **voyageurs** needed canoes large enough to carry heavy loads. They needed canoes that could deliver trade goods to tribal members and could carry many fur pelts back to major trading centers around the Great Lakes.

The **Montreal** Canoe was the largest birchbark canoe. In fact, most Montreal Canoes were thirty to forty feet long, almost twice the size of Native family canoes! They could carry three to four tons of goods and eight or nine voyageurs. The Montreal Canoe was used between Montreal and the western end of Lake Superior. But these large canoes were too heavy to portage and too large to navigate rivers.

Voyageurs at Fort William, about 1860. The fort, also called **Kaministiguia**, was the Hudson's Bay fur trading post.
WHi Image ID 3955

voyageurs (vwah yah **zhurz**): French-Canadian boatmen and traders
Montreal: mon tree **awl**
Kamisnistiguia: kah muh nis tuh **gwee** ah

What Did the Voyageurs Eat?

Voyageurs traded for these Native foods:

- Berries
- Nuts
- **Pemmican**
- Corn
- Wild rice
- Fish
- Dried beans

The smaller and lighter **Nord** Canoe was the answer for moving farther up the smaller rivers, streams, and creeks of the Great Lakes region. The Nord Canoe was about twenty-five feet long and carried only half the **cargo** and half the crew of the Montreal Canoe. But the Nord Canoe could move more rapidly. It could also be portaged around falls or used to navigate smaller rivers.

A good voyageur paddled forty strokes a minute from dawn to dusk. Voyageurs had to unload their goods when it was necessary to portage. They carried bundles that weighed about ninety pounds each. Voyageurs carried these bundles two at a time across a portage.

Sometimes voyageurs needed to make more than one trip carrying cargo during a portage. A voyageur's life was full of adventure but also full of hard work. No wonder these men were known for their big appetites!

Montreal Canoe

The larger Montreal canoe could carry more passengers and cargo, but the smaller Nord canoe could travel into smaller rivers and streams.

Nord: French for "North"
cargo: goods that are carried by ship
pemmican (pem uh kuhn): dried meat, often buffalo

Naming the Great Lakes

Have you ever wondered how the five Great Lakes got their names? When European explorers and voyageurs began to travel the Great Lakes, they learned words from Native languages as they traded with the Native people in the region. Europeans then used Native words to name most of the Great Lakes.

Lake Huron and Lake Erie were named for the local tribes living in the region. The Erie people called themselves "The People of the Panther." Sometimes early French writers called Lake Erie the "Lake of the Cat," because a panther is a large cat.

Lake Ontario was named using a word from the language of the **Iroquois** meaning "beautiful lake."

Ojibwe in the area of Lake Michigan called the lake "**Michigami**," or "big lake." It later became "Michigan."

Lake Superior is the only lake that got its name directly from the early Europeans who explored the area. The French named it "**Lac Superieur**," which means "upper lake," because Lake Superior is at a higher elevation and drains down into the other Great Lakes. The Ojibwe who lived around Lake Superior called the lake "**Gitchigami**," which meant "big water."

The Great Lakes are divided into the lower lakes and the upper lakes. The upper lakes include Lakes Superior, Michigan, Huron, and Erie, while the lower lake is Lake Ontario.

Nord Canoe

Iroquois (ir uh kwoi): a tribe that lived on the shores of Lake Ontario
Michigami: mish uh **gah** mee
Lac Superieur: lahk su pe ray **yur**
Gitchigami: git chee **gah** mee

The Mysterious Disappearance of the *Griffon*

No one knows what the *Griffon* actually looked like, or even how many sails it had. Artists had to make their best guess.
Property of the Kenosha County Historical Society, Inc.

The growing demand for furs created a need for a more **efficient** way of moving these natural resources and goods. The explorers knew they needed a large sailing **vessel** like the ones used to travel across the Atlantic Ocean. But the Niagara Falls prevented ships on Lake Ontario from entering the upper lakes. The upper lakes are the Great Lakes above Niagara Falls: Lakes Erie, Huron, Michigan, and Superior. In 1679, wealthy French fur trader **Robert de la Salle** decided he would build just such a sailing vessel on the Niagara River above the Falls.

This wasn't La Salle's first try at building a ship for the Great Lakes. The year before, he built a vessel called the *Frontenac*. That ship sank in Lake Ontario, above Niagara Falls. He was sure his new ship would succeed. He named it the *Griffon*.

---

efficient (uh **fish** uhnt): not wasting time or energy
vessel: boat or ship
Robert de la Salle: roh **bayr** duh lah **sahl**

On August 6, 1679, La Salle sailed the *Griffon* onto Lake Erie. The *Griffon* headed to a trading post located on an island in Green Bay, Wisconsin, on Lake Michigan. La Salle **disembarked**, and the *Griffon*'s cargo of supplies was unloaded. Then the men loaded the ship with a large cargo of furs. On September 18, 1679, the *Griffon* set sail for Lake Erie. La Salle remained behind. Unfortunately, the *Griffon* and her crew sailed into a violent storm. They disappeared and were never seen again. The *Griffon* was the first ship to sail the upper Great Lakes. It also became the Great Lakes' second shipwreck of a ship built by Europeans—its sister, the **Frontenac**, had sunk the year before. Its location remains a mystery that those who study shipwrecks would love to solve!

University of Wisconsin Cartography Laboratory

disembarked (dis em **bahrkd**): got off
Frontenac: **frohn** tuh nak

Exploration, Not Settlement

The early fur traders and explorers established trading posts and **missions** along waterways. But few French and French-Canadian women and children moved to the region. Some voyageurs and fur traders married Native women and stayed in the region of the Great Lakes. Most of the area remained unchanged. Indians remained in villages scattered throughout the area where they were already living.

The Europeans and French Canadians who came in search of furs did notice other natural resources: forests, **fertile** land, and iron, copper, and lead deposits. Though they did not settle in the Great Lakes region themselves, they told others about these resources and about the natural beauty they had seen.

At first, only a small number of settlers followed the fur traders. Later, large numbers of Europeans and non-Indians born in the United States traveled from areas to the south and east of the Great Lakes. These settlers changed the way people lived in the Great Lakes region. They also changed and found new uses for its waterways.

---

missions: places where people called missionaries shared their religion
fertile (fur tuhl): good for growing crops and plants

Water Routes During the Fur Trade

CANADA

Pigeon River

Lake Superior

Mackinac Straits

Wisconsin River

Green Bay

Wisconsin

Fox River

Mississippi River

Rock River

Lake Michigan

Muskegon River

Tittaba-wassee R.

Michigan

Grand River

Saginaw Bay

Lake Huron

Ottawa River

St. Lawrence River

Lake Ontario

Lake Erie

Illinois River

Wabash River

Ohio River

Missouri River

Key

━━━ Modern border

⇄ Trade route

| 0 | 100 | 200 miles |
| 0 | 100 | 200 kilometers |

University of Wisconsin Cartography Laboratory

4

Fighting for the Inland Seas

Have you ever seen two people who both wanted to do the same thing at the same time? Suppose you and a friend both wanted the last ice cream bar in the freezer on a hot summer day—and neither of you wanted to share. Different groups of people from Europe saw the Great Lakes in the same way. As people came to live in the Great Lakes region permanently, they began to fight over who had the right to take and trade the valuable natural resources found there. And none of these people were thinking about how their fighting would affect the Indians already living there. It took over one hundred years to settle the **conflict** among people from many different nations in the lands that bordered the Great Lakes.

What countries fought over the Great Lakes? Why were they fighting? What was the final outcome of all this fighting? How did the battles over the Great Lakes affect the future of the region, its waterways, and its Native people? You'll find the answers in this chapter.

Europeans Build Forts

In the 1600s and 1700s, the French had moved into Canada, the Great Lakes region, and all the way down the Mississippi River into what is now the state of Louisiana. For a long time only men came to the Great Lakes region and other parts of French North America. They built small forts and trading posts and often married Native women. They lived among the Indians as traders, and they accepted the Native way of life. They did not build settlements of their own.

conflict: fighting

In 1750, the French controlled the parts of the map outlined in green, and the English controlled the parts outlined in orange.
WHi Image ID 42889

Beginning in the 1620s, the British settled all along the eastern edge of North America. Unlike the French, the British brought large numbers of people, including families with men, women, and children. They built towns, farmed the fertile lands, and sometimes traded furs just as the French had done.

The British formed thirteen **colonies** on the coast of the Atlantic Ocean. Native people who had lived in those areas moved—or were forced to move—away from European settlement. Indian people had no choice but to move further west. Because of their contact with white settlers, they brought with them new diseases like **smallpox**. Smallpox killed many Indians in the west, and spread easily. For the most part, the Native people who already lived in the Great Lakes region still controlled that area.

---

colonies: territories settled by people from another country that is still controlled by that country
smallpox: an often deadly disease that causes rash, fever, and blisters that can leave permanent scars

The French and the British were the chief **rivals** in Europe. Their fighting flowed over onto the North American continent. The French and the British fought against one another for almost one hundred years! One reason they fought one another was for control of the North American fur trade. Both sides tried to **recruit** Indian people in the Great Lakes region to fight for their side.

During this long period, French and British settlements in North America slowly grew. The **tensions** between the two groups also grew. The French built more forts along Lake Erie and Lake Ontario. These included forts at **Mackinac**, Niagara, and Detroit. In 1701, French women were finally invited to come to North America. They joined their husbands in Detroit. The French also began to settle on land outside of the forts. This land became farmland.

British traders also reached these lakes. They, too, built a fort on Lake Ontario to protect themselves from the French and to stop their enemies from moving into British-controlled lands and waterways. Each side viewed the other as an **intruder**.

---

rivals (**rɪ** vuhlz): enemies
recruit (ri **croot**): get people to join in fighting
tensions (**ten** shuhnz): bad feelings between people or groups
Mackinac: mak uh naw
intruder: someone who enters in when not invited or welcome

The French and Indian War

The first British ship to sail on the Great Lakes, the *Oswego*, was built in 1755 during the longest of these early wars between the French and the British. This war was known as the French and Indian War. Both sides began building wooden sailing ships to use for trade and for battle. This was the first time the Great Lakes had seen a great number of large vessels on its waters. The Great Lakes have been home to large vessels ever since.

After many years, the British **defeated** the French. In 1760, the British took over all of the land that the French had claimed in Canada and the Great Lakes region. Forts that used to be French were now filled with British soldiers. But the British did not force the French settlers to leave. Despite the British victory, French settlers remained and continued to live there.

In this 1755 battle led by General Edward Braddock, English and Indians fought against the French and lost. Painting by Edwin Deming.
WHi Image ID 1900

British ships are ready to attack the *Oswego* in May 1814 during the War of 1812. Engraving by William Steele.
Collection of Army-Marine and Paul Lear

Oswego: ah **swee** goh
defeated: won in a victory over

But the constant wars had made life in the New World more difficult for everyone living there. Both the French and British were weakened by the resources they had spent and the men they had lost in the wars. The Native tribes lost some of their **independence** to the Europeans. They also lost many of their people to European diseases and conflicts.

How Did the Revolutionary War Affect the Great Lakes?

Not long after the French and Indian War ended, the British citizens of the thirteen colonies in North America became unhappy with how the British government treated them. Many **colonists** wanted to go to the Great Lakes region to farm the fertile land and build their homes. They were angry that the government would not let them move to and settle in the region. Other actions the British government took also made the colonists angry.

In 1775, the colonies decided to fight Great Britain in order to have a greater voice in how the colonies were ruled. But eventually, the colonists wanted complete independence. This fight became known as the **Revolutionary War**. In 1776, the colonists formed their own government.

None of the fighting took place at the few forts in the Great Lakes region. But the Great Lakes did become very important after the fighting ended.

---

independence (in di **pen** duhns): ability to live and move freely
colonists: people who lived in the American colonies
Revolutionary (rev uh **loo** shuh ner ee) **War**: The war in which the 13 American colonies won their independence from Great Britain, from 1775 to 1783

In 1783, the British and the Americans met to talk about their peace agreement. They decided that the Great Lakes would set the border between the United States and Canada. At the time, Canada belonged to the British. Everything south of a line drawn through Lakes Ontario, Erie, Huron, and Superior (including all of Lake Michigan) would be part of the new United States of America. Everything north of that line would be part of Canada. Over two hundred years later, this line still represents the border between the United States and Canada.

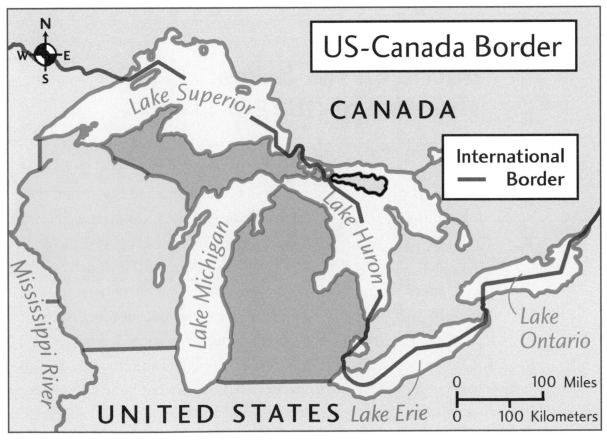

University of Wisconsin Cartography Laboratory

Pioneering Spirit

After the war, the United States government organized what became known as the Northwest **Territory**. This area included what would become Ohio, Michigan, Indiana, Illinois, Wisconsin, and part of Minnesota. Settlers began to move out to the Ohio River and the shores of Lake Erie. Many of the **pioneers** who moved to these areas were people who had fought in the Revolutionary War. The new US government gave them land in the Great Lakes region as a way of saying thank you for fighting to break away from Britain.

Battle on the Lakes: The War of 1812

It was not long before people in the Great Lakes region found themselves involved in a second war between the United States and Britain. The British still controlled Canada and had not yet left their forts in the Great Lakes region. Because of the great distance between Washington, DC, and the Great Lakes, the New US government could not force the British to leave. The people of the United States were angry because the British were still making American sailors serve on British ships. Some British were also encouraging Native people in the Great Lakes region to attack American settlers.

When war broke out in 1812, the Americans and the British both began building big warships on Lake Ontario and Lake Erie to get ready to battle for control of the Great Lakes.

---

territory: area of land that belongs to the United States but is not yet a state
pioneers: the first Europeans to live in a new or unknown area of North America

On September 10, 1813, twenty-eight-year-old **Commodore** Oliver Hazard Perry sailed his **fleet** of nine warships against a British fleet of six ships. For the first two and a half hours of the battle, Perry's **flagship**, the *Lawrence*, did most of the fighting. It was very badly damaged and most of the crew were either killed or wounded.

Oliver Hazard Perry won over the British in the Battle of Lake Erie in 1813. Painting by William Henry Powell.
Perry's Victory. Courtesy of the Ohio Historical Society

---

commodore (**kah** muh dor): an officer in the navy in charge of several ships
fleet: a group of warships under one commander
flagship: the ship carrying the American flag for the rest of the fleet

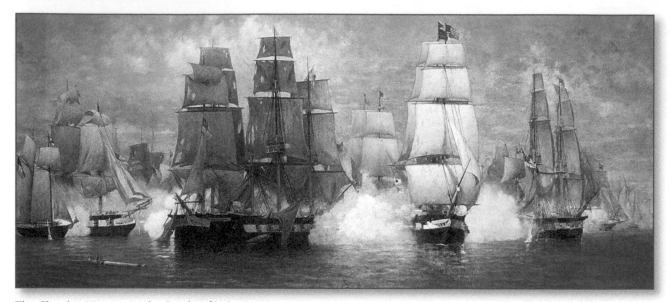

The *Flagship Niagara* in the Battle of Lake Erie
Carol M. Highsmith Archive, Library of Congress, Prints and Photographs Division

Amazingly, Perry was unhurt. But he realized he needed another ship if he was going to beat the British. He got in a small rowboat with four other sailors (and his twelve-year-old brother!) and rowed half a mile to another large American ship, the *Niagara*.

While they rowed, Perry and his men were shot at by British cannons and muskets. Everyone was astonished that none of the shots hit the boat! Perry climbed aboard the *Niagara* with the American flag from the *Lawrence* and once again sailed into the battle. Perry used the powerful guns on the *Niagara* to force the whole British fleet to surrender. He became a hero for the Americans. Sadly, many sailors on both the British and American sides died.

Now that Americans were in control of the Great Lakes, they were able to control the Northwest Territory where they had begun to settle.

Cannons and Guns

The types of weapons that a warship carried was very important. Perry's two largest ships were known as **brigs**. Both of these brigs carried eighteen **carronades** and two **long guns**. Each of the carronades fired a thirty-two-pound iron cannonball. These cannonballs were only the size of a small melon, but they weighed more than two backpacks full of books. Each long gun fired a twelve-pound cannonball. These cannonballs were about as big as a grapefruit, but they weighed as much as a heavy bowling ball. The long guns could fire their cannonballs much farther than the carronade, but the heavier cannonballs fired by the carronade did much more damage. That means that each of Perry's two largest ships could fire up to six hundred pounds of cannonballs at once, more than twice as many as the largest of the British ships could fire.

Long guns were used in battles between sailing ships during the early nineteenth century.
Photo by John Baker, Courtesy Erie Maritime Museum

brigs: sailing ships with two masts and square sails
carronades (ker uh **naydz**): short, stumpy cannons
long guns: cannons that could fire at a great distance

African American Sailors

At this time, many thousands of black men, women, and children were enslaved in the United States. Yet many black sailors fought alongside white sailors in the navy with much less **discrimination** than black Americans faced elsewhere in the United States. In 1813, Congress passed a law that allowed black men who had been born in the United States to join the **military**.

Jesse Williams was one of the African American sailors who fought on the *Lawrence* with Perry. He had also fought in another battle in the Atlantic Ocean and was awarded a silver medal by the state of Pennsylvania for his actions. During the War of 1812, about one in every five soldiers in the US Navy was black.

Why Were Sailing Ships Important to the War of 1812?

The first sailing ships to be used for war on the Great Lakes were built by the British during the French and Indian War. These ships could be used to carry cargo and battle the French. This proved to be a successful combination. After the Revolutionary War, both the United States and Britain continued using sailing ships for carrying cargo and for defense. But it was not until the War of 1812 that both sides realized just how important sailing ships could be.

---

discrimination (dis krim uh **nay** shuhn): unfair treatment of people based on such things as race
military: the armed forces, such as the army and navy
Jesse: jes ee

During the War of 1812, the United States used ships known as **schooners** in their sailing fleets. Some of the schooners were owned by the government, but others were not. Before the country had a large navy, privately owned vessels sometimes served as warships with these fleets. They carried goods or even fought battles. In return, they kept any goods they captured. These ships served as **privateers** for the young United States. The *Hamilton* and the *Scourge* were two schooners that served as warships. Unfortunately, both of these schooners sunk in a sudden and violent **squall** near St. Catherines, Ontario, and ended up as shipwrecks.

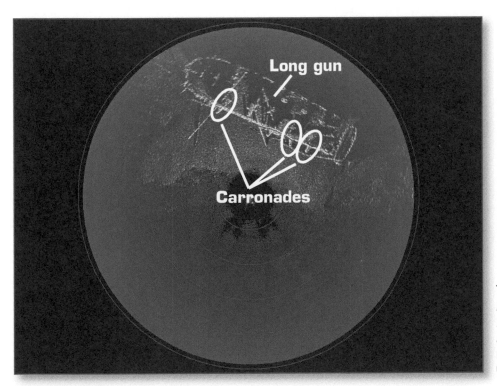

This **sonar image** of the *Hamilton* was taken in 2008, almost 200 years after the ship sank.
Image by ASI Group Ltd., Courtesy City of Hamilton

schooners (**skoo** nurz): fast ships with two masts and sails that run from fore (front) to aft (back)
privateers (prɪ vuh **teerz**): ships hired by the government
squall (skwawl): storm
sonar image: an image created by shooting sound waves at an object through water

Ned Myers, a sailor who survived the sinking of the *Scourge*, described the events. Peaceful one moment, "there not being a breath of air, and no motion to the water," the sky and water around them exploded into a violent storm the next. "A flash of lightning almost blinded me. The thunder came the next instant, and with it a rushing of winds. . . . Our decks seemed on fire, and yet I could see nothing. . . . the schooner was filled with the shrieks and cries of the men to **leeward**, who were lying jammed under the guns, shot-boxes, shot, and other heavy things that had gone down as the vessel fell over. . . . I made a **spring**, therefore, and fell into the water several feet from the place where I had stood. In my opinion the schooner sunk as I left her. I went down some distance myself, and when I came to the surface, I began to swim **vigorously** for the first time in my life."

This ship's **figurehead** is an eagle.
Wikimedia Commons

The story of the *Hamilton* and the *Scourge* has another interesting chapter. In 1973, both ships were rediscovered in over three hundred feet of water at the bottom of Lake Ontario. They were so incredibly well **preserved** that they could be identified by their beautifully carved figureheads. They are some of the oldest shipwrecks found anywhere in the Great Lakes.

---

leeward: the part of the ship that is protected from the weather
spring: jump
vigorously (**vig** ur uhs lee): very strongly
preserved: kept from damage, unchanged
figurehead: a carved figure on the front of a ship

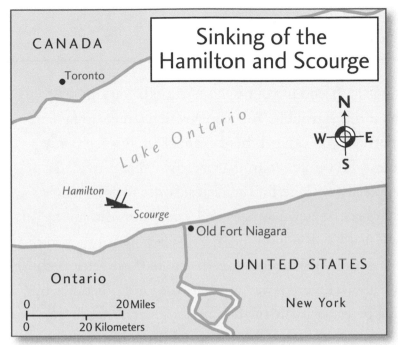

After the war, the Americans and the British decided that the Great Lakes would remain the border between the United States and Canada. They also decided that no fleet of warships could sail on the lakes again. We still respect this decision today.

Years of fighting on the Great Lakes proved the importance of the waterways for those living around them. The end of the War of 1812 brought a final and lasting peace between the United States and Britain. More and more people began settling on the shores of the Great Lakes. And more and more ships were built in the region to move goods and people over their waters.

Most of this new wave of settlement and shipbuilding took place along the borders of Lakes Ontario and Erie. Not long after, people began a huge project to build canals that would link all five Great Lakes. The canals would make it easier to travel to the lands bordering Lakes Huron, Michigan, and Superior. In the next chapter, you will learn more about these projects and how they changed the ways people traveled and traded in the Great Lakes region.

5

Connecting with Canals

If you want to visit a friend in your neighborhood, you can probably get there without much trouble. You know which streets to take. If you know a shortcut, you can get there even faster. It wasn't only French explorers who wanted to find a waterway that provided a "shortcut." People always look for the fastest **route** to get where they are trying to go. In fact, **Yankees** and Europeans did not begin settling in the Great Lakes region in large numbers until they found an easier and faster way to travel there. The route these settlers chose was not really a shortcut, but a way to travel the entire distance by water. Traveling by water made the trip much faster. Once large numbers of newcomers arrived, they changed the entire region and its waterways.

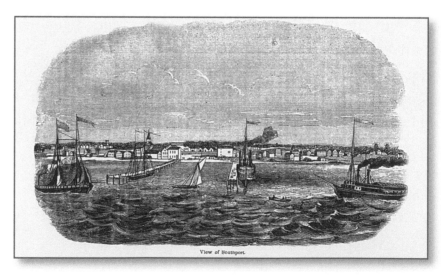

The pier at Southport, Wisconsin, (today known as Kenosha) was a busy place!
WHi Image ID 35754

route (rout *or* root): a familiar path to get from place to place
Yankees (**yang** keez): people from the northeastern United States

What route opened the **gateway** to the Great Lakes region? Who used this route? Where did these newcomers settle? In what ways did their settlements change the region? How did these changes affect our waterways? Read this chapter to find out.

The Push West

Once they were able to travel on the Great Lakes, large numbers of people settled in the region bordering the western Great Lakes— the area now made up of the states of Michigan, Illinois, Indiana, Ohio, Wisconsin, and Minnesota. Much of this area had served as a **crossroads** for Indians and then French fur traders. But the region still remained a long way from the large settlements along the northeast Atlantic coast of the United States.

Many people wanted to move farther west. But travel over land by covered wagon was extremely slow, uncomfortable, dangerous, and expensive. Railroads did not yet exist. Many people at the time still preferred simply to stay where they already lived.

After the American colonists won their independence from the British, many Europeans started to pay more attention to the new nation the Americans had created. More Europeans chose to **immigrate** to the United States. The **immigrants** were looking for better opportunities to raise their families. Their ships anchored in the **harbors** of **port cities** like Boston and New York. These Europeans were moving to the United States to build new lives.

---

gateway: a passage into or out of a place
crossroads: a place where two paths meet
immigrate: permanently move from one country to another
immigrants: people who permanently move from one country to another
harbors: areas of water where sailing vessels can dock and unload their cargo
port cities: towns or cities with harbors

The cities in the Northeast became crowded as more immigrants arrived. Good farmland became harder to find. Many Yankees and immigrants wanted to move to areas with more land, fewer people, and better opportunities for their families. The land along the western Great Lakes looked promising. People just needed an easy way to travel west.

Marine travel proved to be the answer to this problem. The Great Lakes formed natural travel routes once immigrants could reach them. Most immigrant ships docked in the New York City harbor. But what route could people take from there to the Great Lakes and the surrounding territories? The first part of that journey was simple. New York's Hudson River was easy to navigate. The Hudson River took travelers from New York City to Albany, also in New York. But Albany was not on Lake Erie. And Lake Erie was the first of the Great Lakes that people moving west from New York would have to cross.

The Mohawk River flowed between Albany and Buffalo, a city located on Lake Erie. But the Mohawk River was full of waterfalls and rapids. Larger boats carrying many people and their goods could not navigate the river. People needed another way to connect Albany to Lake Erie. If no natural waterway could help, then they would have to *build* a waterway.

The Erie Canal

In the early 1800s, people in New York decided they had to build a canal. A canal promised to be the much-needed shortcut to the fertile lands along and beyond the Great Lakes. Having a canal also meant that once people settled in the Great Lakes region, they could use it to ship their goods and crops back to **markets** in the northeast.

---

markets: places where goods are available for sale

They could even ship them across the ocean to Europe. By July 4, 1817, the building of the Erie Canal was under way.

The actual building of the 325-mile canal took a long time—eight years. It finally opened in October 1825. The boats that traveled up the Hudson were too large to go through the canal. Travelers disembarked at Albany. Then they climbed aboard a smaller canal boat that was **towed** by a team of horses or mules. The animals walked alongside the canal on a special towpath.

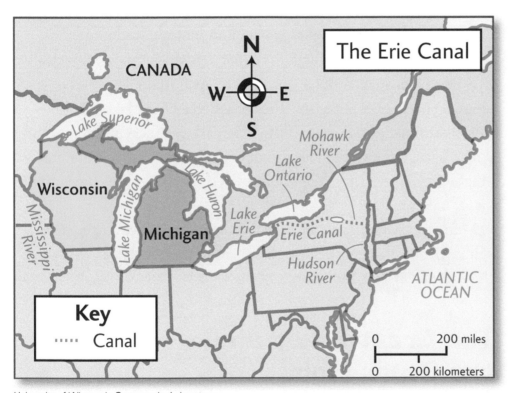

The Erie Canal

University of Wisconsin Cartography Laboratory

---

towed: pulled

In the nineteenth century, horses and mules towed canal boats through the Erie Canal.
Anthony Ravielli

Over the next twenty years, horses and mules towed more than forty thousand boats through the canal. Passengers easily traveled by water from New York City to Buffalo. At Buffalo, they had to change boats again. This time they boarded a larger lake schooner or a **steamboat** to sail west. With New York City serving as the nation's largest port, the Erie Canal became the country's first major "highway," connecting the port cities of the Northeast to the entire Great Lakes region.

Many travelers made their way to the upper Midwest using this route. The opening of the Erie Canal connected the Great Lakes to the Atlantic Ocean and the rest of the world.

The Great Lakes and the Great Eight

There are eight states that border the Great Lakes: Illinois, Indiana, Michigan, Minnesota, New York, Pennsylvania, Ohio, and Wisconsin. Many of those who sailed across the Great Lakes headed for the larger cities in these eight states. Cities like Cleveland,

steamboat: boat powered by a steam engine

The Great Lakes
and the Great Eight

University of Wisconsin Cartography Laboratory

Chicago, Detroit, and Milwaukee grew along the Great Lakes in the days when long-distance travel—for people and for goods—took place by water.

Two other natural resources helped these Great Lakes port cities grow. First, these cities were surrounded by fertile lands. Second, they were located along major rivers that fed into the Great Lakes, places that had been magnets for Native peoples long before Europeans arrived in the region. Chicago and Milwaukee kept the names given to them by the Indians who lived nearby.

Village **sites** and early fur trade centers at Green Bay and Chicago were places of importance to many Native peoples in the Great Lakes region. The present-day cities of **Sault Sainte Marie** and Mackinac, Michigan, were other important trade centers.

sites: locations
Sault Sainte Marie: **soo** saynt muh **ree**

Indian trails that had been used for many, many years also connected these early trading locations. These trails later became the land routes used by the settlers immigrating to the Great Lakes region.

Settlers filled these early trading centers. The trading centers later became villages and towns. The trails and trading routes used to reach them turned into some of the major highways we still use today.

In 1825, the United States invited the Ojibwe, Dakota, and other Indian nations to meet at Prairie du Chien to sign a treaty. This was the first step in getting these tribes to give up their lands. WHi Image ID 3142

Building along the Great Lakes Waterways

Native people had lived and traveled along the Great Lakes and the surrounding waterways for thousands of years. After the Erie Canal opened, the lands that belonged to the Native tribes began to look better and better to people moving west from the northeastern United States and Europe. Unlike the French fur traders, the Yankees and immigrants who arrived after 1830 were coming to stay. They wanted to settle on land that already belonged *to* Native peoples.

Unlike Europeans and European Americans, Native people did not believe that land could be *owned*. Tribal groups did not realize that the **treaties** the US government forced them to sign would give land to the American government *forever*. The government then sold that land to the new settlers. The same treaties that were good for the

treaties: official written agreements between nations

William James Bennett painted the harbor in Detroit in 1836.
Detroit Institute of Arts / The Bridgeman Art Library

new settlers were **tragic** for the Indians who had lived in the areas
opening to American settlement. Native people hated the treaties
that removed them from their homes along the lakes and rivers of
the Great Lakes region. These treaties pushed them to less promising
lands farther west.

The newcomers began to make changes to the places where many
tribes had lived, canoed, and fished for thousands of years. The
settlers changed both the waterways and the surrounding land.

---

tragic: very sad

The kind of settlement that had taken place in many of the larger Great Lakes ports and cities was repeated many times throughout the region as non-Indian newcomers created communities of their own. Like the Great Lakes port cities, some of these new communities grew up where Native villages had once stood. Most of the time, the first changes settlers made to waterways—such as building docks or canals—were designed to improve **navigation**.

People living in port communities also wanted to improve their harbors and rivers. The shallow river bottoms needed to be **dredged** so large boats could travel in and out without getting stuck. Boats traveling along Lakes Michigan, Superior, Huron, Erie, and Ontario also needed harbors that would be safe from stormy waters. Communities needed **piers** to dock incoming schooners and steamers. Finally, since the Erie Canal opened the Great Lakes region to new settlement, many believed that more canals would help people and goods move around and through the area more easily. They argued that if canals could be built at key locations, then people could travel by water *across* the territory between the Great Lakes and the Mississippi River.

Ships coming into the harbor in Milwaukee, about 1853.
WHi Image ID 28081

navigation: guidance of ships from place to place
dredged: scraped the bottom of a body of water to make it deeper
piers (peerz): places to load and unload boats

6

Sail and Steam

Have you ever been in a pool or lake and pushed an **inflatable** boat that had several people in it? Were you amazed at how strong you felt and how easily you could push the boat? The boat's **buoyancy** makes it easy to move. You would never be able to push that much weight around on land. It takes less strength to push or pull a floating object through water than move it across land. This is the reason why water transportation is so much more efficient than land transportation.

We have explored some of the ways people around the Great Lakes have used waterways to travel. Just remember that until the early 1900s, traveling was much easier by water than by land. In fact, it is still more efficient to transport very large amounts of **bulk** goods (such as grain, iron ore, and coal) by water today. Even with railroads, trucks, and airplanes available, waterways still provide the best means of transporting many kinds of goods, especially heavy loads.

More than thirty thousand ships have traveled the Great Lakes. What were some of the most important types? What did they carry? How and why did they change over time? How did people build better ships and change waterways to make water transportation even more efficient?

---

inflatable (in **flay** tuh buhl): able to be blown up with air
buoyancy (**boi** uhn see): ability to float
bulk: in large quantity

In this chapter you will find out that, over time, the **design** of ships changed for several reasons: to go faster, to be safer, to carry more cargo, and to carry different kinds of cargo. Meanwhile, people changed waterways and harbors so that larger ships could navigate the Great Lakes. All of these changes allowed ships to carry more cargo, more quickly. You will also learn to identify some of these boats, from wooden sailing vessels to giant steel ships over one thousand feet long.

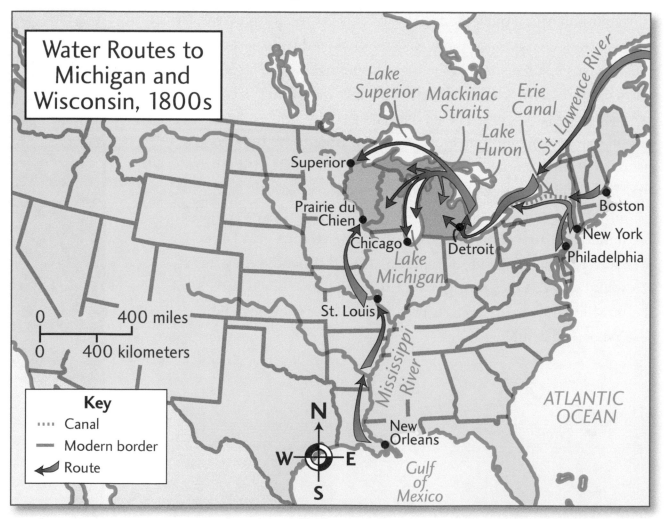

University of Wisconsin Cartography Laboratory

design (di **zin**): shape and style

Early Shipping

Remember the *Griffon*, the first ship built to sail all of the Great Lakes? La Salle knew that a large ship could carry many more furs or trade goods more quickly than the voyageur canoes could. More cargo meant bigger **profits**. The *Griffon*'s **rig** was similar to ships that sailed on the ocean. These ships are called square-rigged vessels (see *Sailing Rigs* on next page).

For some time after the *Griffon* disappeared, only a handful of **commercial** vessels sailed the Great Lakes. But nearly 150 years later, all of that changed. The Erie Canal helped start the shipping **boom** on the Great Lakes that you will read about in this and other chapters. By this time, sailors and shipbuilders learned that fore-and-aft rigged ships (see *Sailing Rigs* on next page) called schooners were better for use on the Great Lakes than square-rigged vessels.

The Great Lakes Schooner

Schooners were ideal for service on the Great Lakes for a number of reasons. First, they were easier and cheaper to build than square-rigged vessels. Second, their sails allowed sailors to **maneuver** these ships, taking advantage of shifting Great Lakes winds more easily than a square-rigger. Finally, since the sails on schooners were easier to handle, these vessels needed fewer sailors. For all of these reasons, schooners were more **profitable** for journeys on the Great Lakes. Naturally, schooners became the most popular vessels for shipping.

---

profits: money made by a business
rig: type of sails and the way these are arranged
commercial (kuh **mur** shuhl): for business
boom: rapid growth
maneuver (muh **noo** vur): steer
profitable: bringing earnings or good outcomes

Sailing Rigs

Square-rigged vessels have sails that hang square from the **mast**. These sails form a line from **port** to **starboard**.

Schooners have two or more masts with fore-and-aft sails. Fore-and-aft sails are fitted along a line that could be drawn from the **fore** of the boat to the **aft** of the boat.

Square-rigged
WHi Image ID 28146

Fore-and-aft-rigged
WHi Image ID 5398

Early schooners were fairly small, generally between fifty and one hundred feet long. The Great Lakes and its harbors had many shallow spots near **shipping lanes**. These shallow areas meant that ships sitting too deep in the water could not navigate safely and sometimes **ran aground**. Because of these problems, Great Lakes vessels were (and still are) built so less of the **hull** is underwater than the hulls of

mast: tall pole sticking up through the boat's deck
port: the left side of the vessel when facing forward
starboard (stahr burd): the right side of the vessel when facing forward
fore: front
aft: rear
shipping lanes: a route regularly used by ships
ran aground: became stuck on a lake or river bottom
hull: the rigid frame and outer shell of a ship

ocean-going vessels. Shallow hulls allow boats to navigate shallow rivers and harbors more safely and with fewer problems.

As Great Lakes shipping became more important, European Americans living in the region felt that the harbors, rivers, and connecting waterways had to be improved to meet the needs of the growing population. They dredged shallow spots and harbors so larger ships could use them. Harbor communities built **breakwaters** to break the force of the waves and provide shelter for ships. Breakwaters also protected the harbors from damage during storms.

This schooner, with its sails hanging to dry, looks like it's sailing through the city! Milwaukee River, about 1870
WHi Image ID 249941

---

breakwaters: low walls placed in the water

How Locks Work

In Chapter 5, you read about the Erie Canal and some early man-made waterways. As time went on and more and more people used canals, these channels began to be built larger so more types of ships could go through. **Locks** were built to help ships get from higher elevations to lower elevations and from lower elevations to higher. Locks allowed vessels to go from one Great Lake to another without switching boats. These canals and locks greatly helped Great Lakes shipping.

Just four years after the opening of the Erie Canal in 1825, the **Welland** Canal opened. The Welland Canal linked Lake Erie with Lake Ontario so ships could navigate between them. Where Lake Erie

Canals and Locks

University of Wisconsin Cartography Laboratory

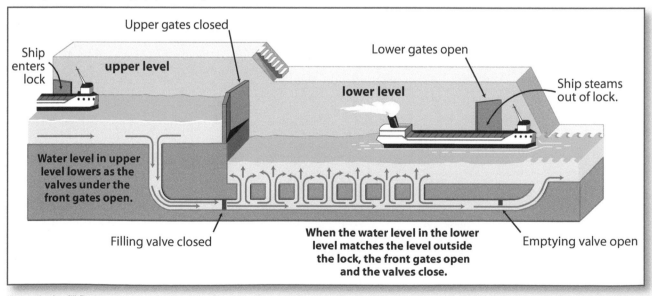

Ship enters lock

Upper gates closed

upper level

Lower gates open

lower level

Ship steams out of lock.

Water level in upper level lowers as the valves under the front gates open.

Filling valve closed

When the water level in the lower level matches the level outside the lock, the front gates open and the valves close.

Emptying valve open

Illustration by Jill Bremigan

---

locks: sections of canals, closed off with gates, used to raise or lower vessels by changing the water level
Welland: wel uhnd

drops into Lake Ontario at Niagara Falls, it drops 326 feet—the height of a skyscraper. The Welland Canal allowed ships to **bypass** the Niagara Falls. It has been enlarged over time and still continues to help ships travel between the Atlantic Ocean and Great Lakes. The Welland Canal allows Great Lakes ports to trade with the world beyond North America.

Lake Superior empties into Lake Huron through Saint Mary's River. Because Lake Superior is twenty-one feet higher than Lake Huron, Saint Mary's River has rapids or falls that prevent ships from navigating between the lakes. The "Soo" Locks at Sault Sainte Marie were built in 1855 so that ships could sail to and from Lake Superior. The Soo Locks lift or lower ships so they can move safely around the rapids between the lakes. The development of northern Wisconsin, Michigan's Upper Peninsula, and Minnesota—in particular the port city of Duluth—depended on the Soo Locks. The Soo Locks allowed these areas to ship grain, fish, lumber, and iron ore to the Northeast and beyond.

A ship passes through the Soo locks, about 1873.
WHi Image ID 96402

The Soo locks today
Whi Image ID 38235

bypass: go around

If a ship did not fit in the canals, there were places it could not travel. Shipbuilders took advantage of the canals and dredging by building ships that would make the best use of the space available in the canals. One such early vessel was a boxy schooner called a **canaler**. The canaler was designed to carry as much cargo as possible and still fit through the Welland Canal. As canals were made larger and shipping channels and harbors were deepened, shipyards built larger ships to carry more goods and make their owners more money.

The number of Great Lakes sailing vessels **peaked** in 1870. At that time nearly two thousand large sailing vessels, most of them schooners, worked the lakes. Large schooners hauled lumber, grain, iron ore, and other goods. Some of these schooners were over two hundred feet long, the length of six school buses! After 1870, however, things began to change. Schooners began to disappear. By the 1900s, there was a more efficient ship people could use—the steamship.

Steam Engines

All sailing ships depend on wind for power. If there is no wind, they cannot sail. If only a light wind is blowing, the sailing ships move very slowly. In the 1800s, shipbuilders wanted a more dependable source of power. The answer was the **steam engine**.

Steam power first appeared on the Great Lakes in the early 1800s. But early steamboats were very expensive to build and to run. Huge steam engines drove giant paddlewheels attached to the sides of these early steamers. The machinery of these sidewheel steamboats took

canaler: cuh **nal** ur
peaked: reached its highest amount
steam engine: an engine that uses the pressure of steam to move its parts

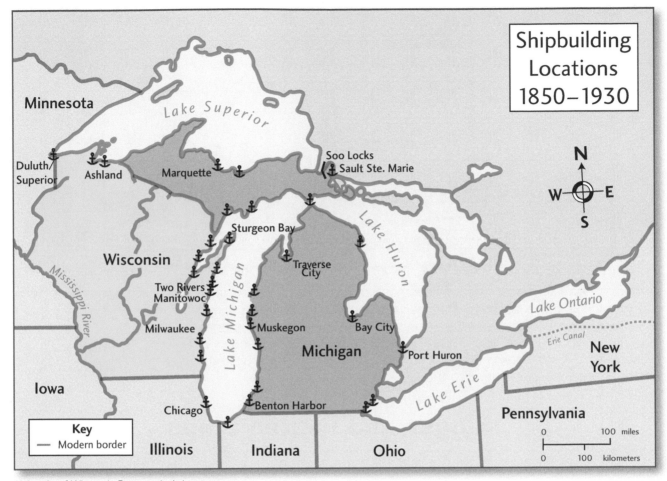

Shipbuilding Locations 1850–1930

Minnesota

Lake Superior

Duluth/Superior
Ashland
Marquette

Soo Locks
Sault Ste. Marie

Lake Huron

Sturgeon Bay

Wisconsin

Lake Michigan

Traverse City

Two Rivers
Manitowoc

Mississippi River

Milwaukee

Muskegon

Bay City

Michigan

Port Huron

Lake Ontario

Erie Canal

New York

Iowa

Chicago

Benton Harbor

Lake Erie

Pennsylvania

Key
— Modern border

Illinois

Indiana

Ohio

N
W   E
S

0   100   miles
0   100   kilometers

University of Wisconsin Cartography Laboratory

up so much space that the ships could not carry as much cargo as a schooner the same size. These early steamboats carried the highest-priced cargo—mainly passengers who bought tickets. In the mid-1800s, more and more Yankees and immigrants wanted to move west, and they looked for the easiest and fastest way possible to travel. The demand for steamboats grew.

Large sidewheel steamships that carried several hundred passengers per trip were built between 1844 and 1857. With fine carpets and expensive decorations, these steamers were known as "palace steamers." The *Western World* and other palace steamers brought many thousands of settlers to the Great Lakes region.
WHi Image ID 63142

Bigger and Faster Ships

From the mid-1880s on, shipbuilders used better materials and techniques to build larger vessels and more efficient engines. Improvements in **technology** resulted in steam engines that took up less space and made ships faster and more powerful. After 1840, some ships were built with **propellers**, instead of the huge sidewheels used on early steamboats. Propellers allowed more space to be used for cargo. This meant that vessels with propellers carried almost as much cargo as a schooner of the same size. They were also cheaper to build and operate than sidewheelers. Steamers now carried all kinds of goods more efficiently than ever before.

technology (tek **nol** oh jee): the use of science and engineering to do practical things
propellers: sets of rotating blades that provide force to move an object through air or water

Hulls made of iron and steel were lighter and stronger. Gradually, they replaced wooden ones. Shipbuilders also designed different types of vessels to haul specific kinds of cargo. The newer vessels carried more and more cargo, traveled faster, and could be loaded and unloaded more quickly than those built earlier. All of these changes resulted in ships that could carry more cargo per trip and make more trips per year. More cargo and more trips made higher profits for the vessels' owners, and cheaper products for customers.

Another type of steamer, the screw steamer or propeller steamer, was introduced in the 1840s. Instead of using paddlewheels, these ships were pushed by a screw propeller or twirling blade at the back of the ship. These propellers looked much like the ones used on powerboats today. Ship owners developed a way to haul lumber cheaply by turning old palace steamers and schooners into barges. Can you see the lumber stacked on the deck of the *Charles H. Bradley*?

Thunder Bay Sanctuary Research Collection

A large steamship, *City of Racine*, sails towards
Milwaukee Harbor loaded with passengers, about 1898.
WHi Image ID 69209

In 1869, the 208-foot *R. J. Hackett* was built specifically to carry grain or iron ore below the deck to keep the cargo dry. The *Hackett* was the first **bulk freighter** on the Great Lakes.
Thunder Bay Sanctuary Research Collection

Steel ships could be built much larger than wooden ships. In the 1880s, steel bulk freighters started to appear on the Great Lakes. The more cargo a ship could carry, the more money it made for its owners. Because of this, the size of new steel ships grew very rapidly.
WHi Image ID 101267

bulk freighter (**fray** tur): a ship designed to carry a great amount of cargo

During 1887 and 1888, Captain Alexander McDougall built his first steam-propelled whaleback in Duluth, Minnesota. He built nineteen more whalebacks over the next ten years to launch in Lake Superior. With rounded sides and a **bow** that looked like a snout, these boats were nicknamed "pig boats." Whalebacks could be built for much less money than other iron ships, but they quickly became outdated because their **hatches** were too small to use new loading equipment. *The Meteor*, which is now a museum in Superior, Wisconsin, is the only whaleback left today.

Wisconsin Department of Tourism

By 1906, steel freighters on the Great Lakes were over six hundred feet long! As bigger canals and locks were built, ships could be built bigger and bigger to fill the locks. That meant every inch of space was available for carrying cargo. The *Edmund Fitzgerald*, which sunk in 1975, is one of the most famous examples of these massive Great Lakes freighters. It was over 720 feet long!

Roger LeLievre

---

bow: front section of a boat

hatches: openings in the deck of a ship, covering the hold where cargo was kept

Great Lakes Shipping Today

Bulk **carriers** still sail on the Great Lakes. These huge ships sail in and out of ports such as Duluth, Sturgeon Bay, Port Huron, and Cleveland. They are powered by **diesel** engines. Some bulk carriers are over one thousand feet long—longer than three football fields! They carry iron ore and coal around the Great Lakes. These thousand-footers are too large to fit through the locks of Welland Canal, so they are "trapped" in the upper lakes. They travel only around the ports of Lakes Superior, Michigan, Huron, and Erie. They can carry over 68,000 tons of cargo—over eighty-two times more than Great Lakes schooners could carry 150 years ago!

What did all this shipping mean for the people who lived and worked in the Great Lakes region? How did the different kinds of ships you have just learned about affect the lives of those people and shape our history? You will learn more about what everyday life in the Great Lakes region was like in the next chapter.

The cargo ship *Tyrone* transports coal on the Menominee River, about 1914.
WHi Image ID 479477

---

carriers: ships that carry commercial goods
diesel (**dee** zuhl or **dee** suhl): a type of fuel oil

Loading and Unloading

As ships became bigger and faster, the gear and techniques used for loading and unloading cargo became more efficient, too. Gravity has always been an important part of the loading process. The easiest way to load a ship is simply to drop the cargo in and let gravity do the work! Over the years, grain and iron ore loaders have developed into huge elevators and slides that can load one-thousand-foot ships in just hours. The same types of improvements were made for unloading ships. These changes helped ships make more trips and more money in the shipping season.

After the invention of a steam-powered shovel called a **Hulett**, one hundred tons of cargo could be unloaded in just minutes.
Library of Congress, Prints & Photographs Division, FSA/OWI Collection, LC-DIG-fsac-1a34840

Hulett: hyoo lit

In the early days of Great Lakes shipping, workers used wheelbarrows and shovels to unload bulk cargo such as coal, iron ore, stone, and grain, unloading about one hundred tons a day.
WHi Image ID 7495

Today, most bulk freighters on the Great Lakes use self-unloading gear. A series of conveyor belts takes cargo from the **hold** to shore. Most Great Lakes bulk freighters can unload thousands of tons of cargo anywhere, without help, in only a few hours!
US Environmental Protection Agency/Great Lakes National Program Office

hold: cargo space inside the ship

7

Sailors and Keepers

The Wind Point Lighthouse in Racine, Wisconsin. Wind Point was supposedly named after a tall tree on that was a familiar sight to sailors on Lake Michigan.
Library of Congress, Prints & Photographs Division, photograph by Carol M. Highsmith, LC-DIG-highsm-12135

In Chapter 6, you learned that thirty thousand vessels traveled the Great Lakes. You learned about schooners, steamers, and freighters—how they were built and how they were powered. Chapter 7 looks at the people who were on the ships and the safety measures used to protect them from danger.

Traveling on the Great Lakes can be dangerous. Storms, fog, **shoals**, and **treacherous** shorelines make piloting a vessel a difficult job. Today, ship pilots use aids to navigation such as computers, advanced weather tracking, and **GPS** devices to avoid danger. Even with all of that equipment, ships sometimes end up in trouble. Imagine you were sailing a ship one hundred years ago before this helpful equipment was invented. You would have to rely on **charts**, which were not always available, on your sailor's

shoals: shallow sandbars
treacherous (**trech** ur uhs): full of hidden dangers
GPS: Global Positioning System, a device that tells your exact location based on signals from satellites
charts: maps of the sea that give routes for traveling

instincts, and on lighthouse lamps and **fog horns** to guide you safely to your destination.

What kind of person joined the crew of a ship? What were the responsibilities of the crew? How did lighthouse keepers and lifesaving stations protect sailors? How did lighthouses work, and who took care of them? In Chapter 7, we will answer these questions about the people who worked on ships and those on shore who worked to protect them.

The Sailor's Life

The ships traveling the Great Lakes carried a lot of cargo. A ship needed a good crew to successfully load a vessel's cargo, travel with it, and unload it. Great Lakes schooners hired many sailors who came from distant countries. They crossed the Atlantic Ocean bringing old **seafaring** skills. They worked side by side with people born in the Midwest who had never seen saltwater but understood the lakes. In 1860, there were so many immigrant sailors that only one out of every five sailors living and working out of the port

A fleet of lumber schooners, including the *Vega* and the *Ottawa*, docked in Charlevoix, Michigan, about 1898
WHi Image ID 5583

city of Chicago had been born in the United States. No matter their differences, a crew had to pull together to survive in a storm.

---

instincts: knowledge that comes without thinking or studying
fog horns: horns for sounding warning signals in fog or darkness
seafaring: having to do with sailors or the sea

Life on a Great Lakes schooner required sailors to develop special skills. It was a special way of life. Not only was it different from working on land, but sailing on the Great Lakes was also very different from working on the ocean. Crews on Great Lakes schooners worked **seasonally**. In early spring they set sail as soon as the ice melted away from the Great Lakes. They worked on the schooners through the hot summer and into the cold days of early December, or until ice once again blocked the waterways.

Great Lakes sailors also had to deal with rough living conditions. Most of the sailing season was bitterly cold and windy. The hardy crews sailed through terrible storms and murky fogs. On a Great Lakes schooner, people shared a very small living space because most of the vessel was filled with cargo. The captain, **mate**, and cook lived in a stuffy cabin at the back end of the ship. Common sailors slept at the extreme forward end of the ship, in a dark wedge of space below deck called the **fo'c'sle**. Terribly hot in the summer and bone-chillingly cold in the fall and winter, schooners stayed damp or wet most of the time.

The crew would spend their days keeping watch, steering the ship, and pulling on lines to adjust the sails. When in port they hauled up the anchor by cranking on the **windlass** in the bow and helped to load and unload cargo. Sailors also spent a lot of time taking care of their ship—scraping, painting, scrubbing the deck, and making repairs to the ship and sails.

A schooner crew
Thunder Bay Sanctuary Research Collection

seasonally: with the seasons
mate: officer right below the captain
fo'c'sle (fohk suhl): small living space under the bow where the crew was housed
windlass (wind luhs): a tool that raises or lowers an anchor

While raising the sails or anchor, the crew might join in singing sea **shanties**, which would help them work together as a team or keep up good spirits on a long or difficult trip.

Wind and muscle powered the schooners of the Great Lakes. Food fueled the crew members who worked hard pulling lines, climbing rigging, and handling cargo. The fertile coastlines of the Midwest, Great Lakes schooners supplied crews with lots of fresh produce and fish. Good food in the ship's **galley** helped attract a good crew. Great

The crew dining room on the *Nyanza*, a bulk freighter built in Michigan in 1890. The man in the photo is the ship's **steward**.
Thunder Bay Sanctuary Research Collection.

Lakes sailors also enjoyed endless fresh water. For the many sailors who began their careers on the Atlantic Ocean, this water proved to be a real treat; on the salty ocean, fresh water was rare.

The galley served up food and also offered opportunities. Women and African American men, two groups with limited job opportunities on land during these years, often served as cooks on schooners. Probably more women worked on sailing ships in the Great Lakes during the 1870s and 1880s than anywhere else in the world. But the work was hard and dangerous. Cooks had to feed people that worked around the clock while the schooner was constantly moving.

---

shanties: sailor's songs
steward: a person who serves passengers and crew on a ship
galley: ship's kitchen

Blow the Man Down
Author Unknown

I'll sing you a song, a good song of the sea
With a way, hey, blow the man down
And trust that you'll join in the chorus with me
Give me some time to blow the man down

There was an old skipper I don't know his name
With a way, hey, blow the man down
Although he once played a remarkable game
Give me some time to blow the man down

His ship lay be-calmed in the tropical sea
With a way, hey, blow the man down
He whistled all day but in vain for a breeze
Give me some time to blow the man down

This sea shanty describes life aboard a sailing ship, where tensions ran high and fistfights were not uncommon. "Blow the man down" means to beat another sailor in a fight.

Lighthouses

Because sailing the Great Lakes was dangerous, people did what they could to help ships travel safely. During storms, fog, and the dark of night, ships needed a **beacon** of light to help guide them. The first lights on the lakes were not in lighthouses. They were simply large fires built up on high points of land. These fires were difficult for ships to see, but even this much light was helpful for a ship captain.

Lighthouses in the United States began appearing as early as 1716 along the Atlantic coast, a time when the Great Lakes region was vast wilderness. As settlers later arrived in the Great Lakes region, boat traffic increased. The first two lighthouses on the Great Lakes were built in 1818 at Buffalo, New York, and Erie, Pennsylvania. The oldest lighthouse on the Great Lakes that is still being used today is Ohio's Marblehead Lighthouse. It was built in 1822.

After the Erie Canal was built in 1825, more ships began sailing the Great Lakes than ever before. The discovery of copper in the 1840s in Michigan's Upper Peninsula,

---

beacon: signal

along with the opening of the Soo Locks in 1855, meant more ships than ever were travelling on the Great Lakes. Increased shipping meant a greater need for safety.

The US Lighthouse Service and the US Lifesaving Service (now combined as the US Coast Guard) were created to protect and serve the ships and sailors on the Great Lakes. The shores became dotted with many lighthouses.

The lights and horns guided sailors on their voyages by marking specific points of land, islands, entrances to harbors, and dangerous **reefs**. By 1877, there were 143 lighthouses on the Great Lakes kept by hardworking lighthouse keepers and their families. In all, 220 lighthouses were constructed on the US shores of the Great Lakes. Door County in Wisconsin has twelve of the state's thirty-five lighthouses. Marblehead Lighthouse in Ohio is the oldest lighthouse on the Great Lakes that is still in use today. Michigan has had ninety lighthouses built along its miles of shoreline—more than any state in the entire country.

The Marblehead Lighthouse on Lake Erie
Photo by John McCarty

reefs: shallow areas of rocks or sand

You can see that Michigan is bounded by water on most of its borders.

University of Wisconsin Cartography Laboratory

US Lifesaving Stations

A lighthouse is a tower, sometimes tall, sometimes short, that gives off light using lamps with special **lenses**. Around the lighthouse are other necessary outbuildings, such as the keeper's house, fuel house, and boathouse. Sometimes a lighthouse keeper would use the station's boat to venture out in stormy weather to save shipwreck survivors.

Often near very dangerous waters, a lifesaving station was built to house people who were specially trained to rescue shipwreck survivors. These men, and sometimes women, were ready in storms or fog to rescue sailors and passengers from wrecked ships. Lifesaving crews were very brave, made many daring rescues, and worked at great risk to their own personal safety. In places where lighthouses could not be built, such as over treacherous reefs or areas too far offshore for a lighthouse's lens to reach, lightships were anchored. These lightships had a beacon light just like a lighthouse to help guide and warn ships. Today, the US Coast Guard patrols the Great Lakes, ready to help in an emergency.

The lightship *Peshtigo*
Wisconsin Maritime Museum Collection

A lifesaving crew at work near Two Rivers. The *Francis Hinton* is wrecked in the background.
Wisconsin Maritime Museum Collection

---

lenses: curved pieces of glass

Edith Morgan

One hero of a lifesaving station on Lake Michigan was Edith Morgan, the young daughter of the station's keeper at Grand Point au Sable. The steamer *City of Toledo* wrecked in late December 1879, after the summer lifesaving crew was gone for the season. Edith spent many hours in the freezing water and snow alongside other volunteers who lived nearby. She and the men used a long line of rope stretching from the ship to the shore to pull the stranded crew off the ship. The year before, Edith had jumped into a lighthouse rescue boat with her father in an attempt to reach another stranded ship. She was awarded a silver lifesaving medal for her heroic actions.

Lighthouse Keepers

Taking care of a lighthouse was a big job. Lighthouse keepers were almost as important as the lighthouse itself. Without them, the lighthouse would not be able to run. Without the lighthouse running, ships and all those on board faced possible danger.

Of course, the most important job was to keep the lighthouse lamp burning. In the 1800s, a lamp was made with a wick that rested in a container of oil. The keeper would light the wick with a match. The lighthouse keeper had to make sure the container of oil was kept full to keep the flame burning. But how were sailors on the Great Lakes able to see such a tiny flame? Lenses were placed around the light to make the light look bigger and brighter. Lighthouse keepers kept the lenses clean and replaced them when they broke. Today, lighthouses are powered with electric lights, and don't need as much **upkeep** as they did in the past.

Sounding the foghorn was another important task for the lighthouse keeper. When a fog rolled in, the mechanical horn had to be sounded. To sound the horn the lighthouse keeper had to wind the **clockwork**. In an emergency, if the horn was not working, the lighthouse keeper used a bell. Sometimes a fog would settle in for two days. Ringing a bell for two days was a tiring job! As time went on foghorns became more advanced. In the 1900s most foghorns were powered by diesel engines or electric motors.

---

upkeep: making sure something works well
clockwork: mechanical device made of wheels with teeth

Lenses placed around a lighthouse's lamp allowed sailors on the Great Lakes to see the flame better by making it look bigger and brighter.
Library of Congress, Prints & Photographs Division, HAER, HAER MINN,38-TWOHA.V,1-11 (CT)

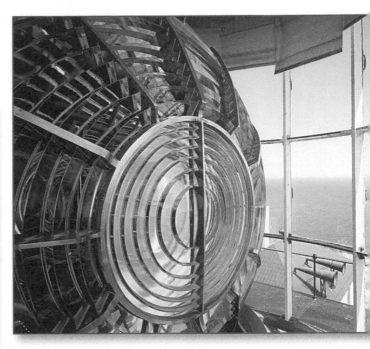

The Split Rock Lighthouse and Foghorn in Two Harbors, Minnesota. The lighthouse was built after a powerful storm in November 1905.
Library of Congress, Prints & Photographs Division, photograph by Carol M. Highsmith, LC-DIG-highsm-12124

Lighthouse keepers had to keep the lighthouse in good working order. Because most lighthouses were **isolated**, the keeper had to be able to do a lot of different jobs. Lighthouse keepers had to be skilled as builders, plumbers, electricians, and more.

---

isolated: set apart from others

Lighthouse Families

Many lighthouses were built in areas so dangerous only the lighthouse keeper could live there. But others were located in areas that were not quite so dangerous or isolated. When this was the case, the lighthouse keeper did not live alone. His family joined him, and even pets came along.

Lighthouse families often found lighthouse living a unique experience. It was not like living in town, on a farm, or even in the woods. Lighthouses were built on islands or peninsulas or in areas that might be many miles from other homes. Things you might take for granted—playing with friends, getting goods from the local store, or even going to school—were a challenge for the lighthouse keeper's family.

South Manitou Island Lighthouse off the coast of Michigan
Library of Congress, Prints & Photographs Division, HABS, HABS MICH, 45-GLAR,8A-4

To keep from getting lonely, children had to create their own entertainment. Brothers and sisters became best friends and classmates. When the weather was nice they played outside, had picnics, walked on the beach, or climbed over rocks. Growing up on North Manitou Island in Lake Michigan, Glenn Furst and his brother made kites and wooden boats out of driftwood and bird feathers.

When the weather wasn't so nice, children played inside. Most lighthouses had their own small library, so reading was a popular pastime. Reading became so popular that in the late 1800s, the Lighthouse Association began its own library program. Books were delivered by boat to the most isolated lighthouses. Knot tying and games like dominoes and checkers also kept children busy. Derrick Simonson grew up in the South Superior Entry Lighthouse. When he was young, he would sit for hours watching the ships pass by. He made up his own game trying to guess what type of ships they were and which company they worked for.

Chores and odd jobs also kept children busy. Most of the chores were done alongside their parents. Unlike people working at many other jobs, lighthouse keepers and their families lived, slept, and ate where they worked. In the kitchen, there was cooking, canning, cleaning, and mending clothes. In the tower, there was keeping the light lit and making small repairs. Outside there was wood to be chopped, food to be gathered, and much more. During warmer seasons, many lighthouse families kept a garden. It was hard for these families to get to town for fresh fruits and vegetables, so they grew their own. For milk and cheese, many families kept cows or goats. Other forms of protein, like fish, were easy to get. The keeper and his family only had to cast a line into the lake.

Because lighthouses were often located in isolated and dangerous areas and the keeper and his wife were often busy, the children sometimes found themselves in less-than-safe situations. When playing, they had to be careful of steep, rocky areas, large waves, and cold water. Parents often worried about their children drowning. Sometimes, adults would attach a rope harness around the littlest children. The harness was then tied to the house to make sure the child couldn't wander too far.

Even with **precautions** in place, accidents happened. When Ella Luick's lighthouse keeper husband, **Emmanuel**, got sick in November 1901, Ella ran the station at Sand Island.

---

precautions (pri **kaw** shuhnz): actions taken to prevent danger
Emmanuel: i **man** yoo uhl

Thunder Bay Island Lighthouse

The Thunder Bay Island Lighthouse on Lake Huron was so isolated that, in general, the lighthouse keeper was the only person you would find living there year-round. There was one exception. From 1877 to 1915, John Persons was the lighthouse keeper. His wife, **Cecilia**, and their two children, Byron and Nina, decided to stay at the lighthouse with John. Cecilia was a smart, strong woman. She was able to care for her family and provide her children with an education. In the middle of winter, the only way to get to town was to sail across the ice. John and Cecilia used a boat with skis attached to the bottom.

As their children grew, Cecilia began to help John more and more with the lighthouse. She also helped with the nearby lifesaving station. The lifesaving station was occupied only during the warmer months of the year. This was a problem because accidents happened all year round. Cecilia's hard work at the lighthouse, the lifesaving station, and the well-being of the sailors made her a good choice for a lifesaving job. In order to work at the lifesaving station, however, she needed to be able to captain a boat. So Cecilia Persons became the first woman on the Great Lakes to become a captain.

Thunder Bay Island Lighthouse
Thunder Bay Sanctuary Research Collection

When they were ready to leave for winter, she wrote in the lighthouse log, "Mrs. Luick inspected the Station. Everything in order for the winter." In 1832, when Rachel Wolcott's husband died, she took over the lighthouse in Marblehead, Ohio. She managed the light equipment, performed the lifesaving duty of warning ships of the dangers along the coastline, and took care of her children at the same time.

The Great Lakes region grew rapidly. Many different kinds of people from many different places flocked to the shores of the Great Lakes.

Cecilia: suh **seel** yuh

The US Coast Guard still uses ships like the *Mackinaw* for search and rescue and for breaking up ice. Here, the *Mackinaw* patrols very icy waters in Whitefish Bay, Wisconsin.

U.S. Coast Guard photo/Petty Officer 3rd Class George Degener

They worked hard and made new lives for themselves and their families. In the late 1800s and early 1900s, people flowed into the region while natural resources like iron ore and lumber flowed out. Such changes made the Great Lakes richer and busier than ever before. A busy Great Lakes made it a successful time for the shipping industry as well.

Lighthouses and lifesaving stations played a significant role in that industry. The lighthouse light and foghorn guided many vessels and their sailors safely through dangerous areas. However, with so much shipping in the region, shipwrecks also became more common. Some ships ran into storms, ran aground, or **collided with** other vessels. The individuals who worked the lifesaving stations did their best to rescue the sailors. In the next chapter, you will learn about some of the dangers ships faced on the Great Lakes, what happened to the ships that didn't make it, and what they can tell us about the ones that did.

collided with: ran into

8

Shipwrecks

The bow of the *Fedora* rises up from
Lake Superior's floor.
Photo by Tamara Thomsen, Wisconsin Historical Society

You learned earlier in this book that as soon as people settled in the Great Lakes region, they began to travel on its lakes and rivers. If you added up all of the voyages that took place from that time until now, the number would be in the millions. Most of these individual voyages across the Great Lakes were successful, but accidents could and did happen. Storms, fog, human mistakes, broken machinery, and fires sometimes caused vessels to sink. Nobody knows just how many boats, ships, and Indian canoes have sunk on the Great Lakes. Most likely, many thousands.

The "Shipwreck Century"

The majority of those shipwrecks occurred during what we will call the "Shipwreck Century," a period between 1825 and 1925. The Shipwreck Century took place during the time when millions of people moved from the East Coast to the Midwest. As you learned earlier, many of these newcomers traveled over the Great Lakes to get to the places that became Michigan, Wisconsin, Illinois, Indiana, Minnesota, and Ohio. As more people came to settle in this part of the country, they needed food, lumber, and other supplies that they couldn't find near their new homes. These supplies needed to be shipped to the Midwest. Soon, the region's plentiful natural resources, such as lumber from the forests and minerals from the ground, were being shipped from the Midwest to faraway places. With all these people and things on the move, more ships than ever were sailing on the Great Lakes!

There are hundreds of shipwrecks in the Great Lakes waiting to be explored.
Photo by Tamara Thomsen, Wisconsin Historical Society

Most of the ships that sailed during the Shipwreck Century were lucky. They made it to and from ports in many cities time and time again, bringing valuable cargoes like wheat, iron, or coal from one side of the Great Lakes to the other. However, some ships were not as lucky. The ships that didn't make it are often left behind as shipwrecks. Shipwrecks can be found throughout the Great Lakes. They lie in the sand along the shorelines, scattered among the rocks in shallow areas, or on the bottom in hundreds of feet of water.

Why did so many ships sink in the Great Lakes during the Shipwreck Century? What are some of the shipwrecks that happened close to Wisconsin and Michigan? What can shipwrecks tell us about the ships that sank? Where did they come from? What were they doing before they sank? You will find the answers to these questions in this chapter.

Shipwreck Alley

Certain areas of the Great Lakes were particularly **hazardous** for ships during the Shipwreck Century. Thunder Bay, located along the northwest coast of Lake Huron, is one of those dangerous areas. More shipwrecks were left behind in Thunder Bay than in many safer areas around the Great Lakes. In fact, there are over two hundred shipwrecks in and around the Thunder Bay area. That's why it's known as a "shipwreck alley."

Imagine that you are a sailor on a Great Lakes schooner a little more than one hundred years ago. It is a night in late November, very dark and very cold. You are sailing through the night, trying to get

---

hazardous (**haz** ur duhs): dangerous

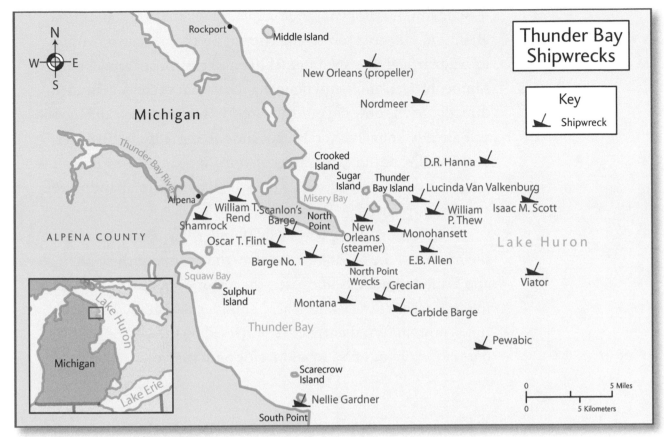

University of Wisconsin Cartography Laboratory

the very last shipment of grain for the season up to Buffalo, New York. By now, your ship should be passing by the southern tip of Thunder Bay Island, a small island just off the coast of northeastern Michigan.

But the waters out on Lake Huron are covered in such a thick, dense fog that you can just barely make out the light from the nearby lighthouse. You strain your eyes, trying to spot shoals and reefs. You hope your ship can make it through the fog without running aground in the shallow waters you know are out there somewhere.

Suddenly, it is not your eyes but your *ears* that are standing at attention. You hear something else out on the lake, also making its way through the icy water. The sound gets closer and closer. Moments later, another schooner appears out of the fog, headed directly for the bow of your ship! You yell to alert the captain, but you already know it is too late for the two big ships to turn and avoid hitting one another. You can only hope that when this other schooner collides with yours, you will all be able to **abandon** your sinking ship safely.

The collection of shipwrecks in Thunder Bay is very important to the history of the Great Lakes region, the history of the United States and Canada, and, in some cases, the histories of other countries in other parts of the world. These Thunder Bay shipwrecks are so important, in fact, that they are protected by the US government as part of the Office of National Marine **Sanctuaries**.

Thunder in Thunder Bay: The *Isaac M. Scott*

The Great Lakes are known for having dangerous weather, and Thunder Bay is no **exception**. You can tell from the name itself! Even today, with technology that allows us to predict the weather and easily look up forecasts, fogs and storms can still seem to pop up out of nowhere on the Great Lakes. Sailors during the Shipwreck Century didn't have these technological advantages. Weather created a big problem for ships sailing during that time.

---

abandon: to leave behind with no plan to return
sanctuaries: places of safety and refuge
exception (ek **sep** shuhn): different from the rest

Thick fogs meant low **visibility**, which could cause ships to run aground in shallow areas or collide with other ships. Heavy storms created howling winds that could make sailing ships impossible to control. Enormous waves could flood a ship's deck and cargo holds. Many ships that sailed late in the year were trying to make a little more money with one last run across the lakes. These ships were the most likely to run into freezing winter weather that could badly damage them or cause them to become trapped in ice.

In November 1913, many ships were lost during one of the biggest storms ever seen on the Great Lakes. The "Great Storm of 1913" was especially bad on Lake Huron. Eight ships sank, and over two hundred sailors died during that one storm alone. One of the lost ships was the *Isaac M. Scott*, a steel bulk freighter built in 1909.

The *Isaac M. Scott*, a bulk freighter built in 1909, sunk in Lake Huron during the great storm of 1913.
Ken Thro Collection, Lake Superior Maritime Collections, UW–Superior

visibility (viz uh **bil** uh tee): the ability to see

The *Isaac M. Scott* was a real giant—504 feet long. She was built to carry loads of over ten thousand tons of coal and iron ore. Even an enormous ship built of sturdy steel like the *Isaac M. Scott* was no match for the Great Storm of 1913.

Out on the lakes during that storm, sailors faced sudden, blinding snow storms and waves as tall as thirty-five feet. Gusts of wind reached ninety miles per hour. The *Isaac M. Scott* was struggling to make her way through the horrible storm with her cargo of coal when the ship was hit by a wave so large it rolled the ship right over. Once the ship was upside down and flooded with water, the *Isaac M. Scott* sank into the icy November water with all the crew still on board. The shipwreck of the *Isaac M. Scott* can still be found at the bottom of Lake Huron, resting upside down.

Shallows and Shoals: The *New Orleans*

Bad weather was probably the most common reason that ships wrecked in Thunder Bay, but sailors could also find themselves in trouble on perfectly clear, calm days. Even when the surface of the lake is smooth, shallow reefs and rocky shoals lie hidden all along the shorelines of Thunder Bay. When a ship sails into a shallow area, its bottom can get stuck in the rocks or sand on the bottom. Sometimes the ships can be pulled backward off these reefs or shoals and back into deeper water. Other times, the ship is so damaged by hitting the rocks or sand that it can't be rescued.

Today, detailed **nautical** charts warn navigators of these shallow areas to help prevent ships from running aground. The charts are

---

nautical (**naw** tuh kuhl): having to do with the sea, sailing, or sailors

The *New Orleans* ran onto a reef at Sugar Island on June 14, 1849. Strong winds and waves destroyed the stranded vessel a few days later.
Thunder Bay Sanctuary Research Collection

updated using the latest technology to detect the dangers that lie on the sea floor. Back in the Shipwreck Century, however, sailors could often only guess where they might be able to make their way safely through the reefs surrounding Thunder Bay. Ships that guessed incorrectly or that lost control during storms are the ones that have ended up as shipwrecks in the Thunder Bay National Marine Sanctuary.

The *New Orleans* is the oldest known shipwreck in the Thunder Bay National Marine Sanctuary. The *New Orleans* was a sidewheel palace steamer that carried passengers across the Great Lakes after they had traveled up the Erie Canal. This 185-foot-long steamer was heading through Thunder Bay early on a foggy morning, June 13, 1849. Without warning, the *New Orleans* ran aground on a reef between North Point and Sugar Island. Luckily, local fishermen saw the ship wreck and were able to rescue all of the passengers and crew aboard.

Orleans: or luhnz or or **leenz**

The ship, however, was not so lucky. It was badly broken up on the reef and could not be saved. Because the ship ran aground in shallow water, today the shipwreck of the *New Orleans* lies in only fifteen feet of water and can be seen from the surface. This makes it a great place to visit for people who like to **snorkel** or **kayak** in Thunder Bay.

Crowded Shipping Lanes: The *Pewabic*

Shipping lanes in the Shipwreck Century were like the crowded highways of today. The traffic was fast and heavy. Ships traveled in more than one direction along these routes through the water. Some shipping lanes, like northern Lake Huron near Thunder Bay, had dozens of ships sailing through at any one time. Unlike cars on modern highways, however, ships sailing during the Shipwreck Century didn't have streetlights, marked lanes, or signs to guide their way.

During the Shipwreck Century, charts did not have as many details about possible dangers in the Lakes as they have today. Ships powered by sails were harder to control and harder to navigate. Navigators didn't have the advantage of technological aids like radios. Such aids would have allowed them to know where other ships were and where they could safely sail to avoid one another. Mistakes made by those in charge of the large ships that sailed the Great Lakes could cost shipowners lots of money and property, and in the worst case, people's lives.

---

snorkel (**snor** kuhl): swim close to the surface of water using a special tube that lets you breathe
kayak (**kı** ak): paddle a slim, light boat with pointed ends

Bad luck put the *Pewabic* and *Meteor* in each other's paths.
Painting by Robert McGreevey, NOAA, Thunder Bay National Marine Sanctuary

The lakes were calm and only a light mist was falling on the evening of August 9, 1865. Two **sister ships**—the *Pewabic* and the *Meteor*—were traveling the shipping lanes of Lake Huron. Built in 1863, the *Pewabic* was a screw-propeller steamer, two hundred feet long, with two engines and a smoke stack. Both ships were carrying passengers and valuable cargo. The cargo on the *Pewabic* consisted of over two hundred tons of copper, seventy-five tons of iron ore, and barrels of fish. Just after passing by Thunder Bay Island, the *Pewabic* caught sight of the *Meteor*. The two ships were about six miles apart and could see one another clearly. It was common for passing ships to trade news and mail from opposite sides of the lake.

---

sister ships: ships with the same design
Pewabic: puh **wah** bik

A **photomosaic** shows the wreck of the *Pewabic* from above.
NOAA, Thunder Bay National Marine Sanctuary

However, this meant that they had to get very close to one another, sometimes dangerously close.

On this night, as the ships got closer to one another, the *Pewabic* unexpectedly cut across the path of the *Meteor*. The *Meteor* slammed into the *Pewabic*, putting a deep hole in the ship. The *Pewabic*'s bow began to flood, raising her stern up out of the water. As the ship tipped forward, the heavy cargo it was carrying slid forward. The cargo's movement forced the ship to sink even faster.

Some of the passengers aboard the *Pewabic* managed to jump onto the deck of the *Meteor* or into the chilly water. Others never made it off of the ship. The passenger list sank along with the *Pewabic*, but we do know that at least thirty-three people—6 crewmen and 27 passengers—drowned in Thunder Bay that night, all because of a terrible mistake. The shipwreck of the *Pewabic* rests out in the deep waters of Thunder Bay, 165 feet below the surface. In the decades that followed, many attempts were made to **salvage** the ship's valuable cargo of copper—and many divers died in the attempt. Until technology caught up and diving became safer, the wreck of the *Pewabic* had a reputation for being deadly, years after it had sunk.

---

photomosaic (**foh** toh moh **zay** ik): a picture that is made up of many smaller pictures
salvage: to get cargo from a shipwreck

Fire! The *Montana*

Most ships that sailed during the Shipwreck Century were built completely out of wood. Wood is a great building material and has been used to build ships for thousands of years. But wood is also **flammable**. Over the course of the Shipwreck Century, more and more ships began to use steam engines instead of sails. Although steam engines made ships faster and more efficient, they also made fire an even bigger risk.

Steam engines required ships to have boiling hot furnaces down below their wooden decks. Locating the furnaces directly under the flammable decks presented an added danger for the cargo, passengers, and crew. This very dangerous combination caused a number of ships to burn in Thunder Bay.

The *Montana* caught fire with a full load of lumber.
Library of Congress, Prints & Photographs Division, Detroit Publishing Company Collection, LC-D4-13084

flammable: able to be burned

The wooden steamer *Montana* was 236 feet long. It traveled on the Great Lakes for more than forty years, carrying all kinds of cargo back and forth. After years of working on the Great Lakes, the ship was coated in layers of paint, oils, and coal dust. This made the whole ship very flammable. On September 6, 1914, a fire started in the bow of the *Montana* and then spread quickly to the rest of the ship. The crew managed to escape in their lifeboat, but the ship burned and eventually sank. Now, all that is left of the *Montana* are the parts of the ship that were below the water when it burned. This shipwreck lies in sixty feet of water. The huge timbers from the bottom of the hull and the massive three-story steam engine and its great boilers now are home to fish. Wrecks like the *Montana* are also great places for divers to visit.

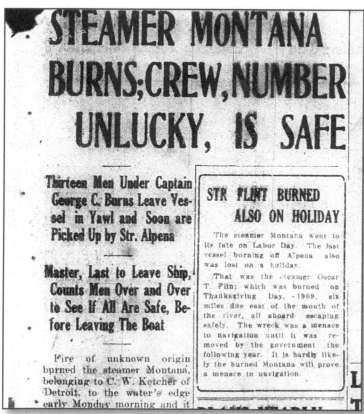

STEAMER MONTANA BURNS; CREW, NUMBER UNLUCKY, IS SAFE

Thirteen Men Under Captain George C. Burns Leave Vessel in Yawl and Soon are Picked Up by Str. Alpena

Master, Last to Leave Ship, Counts Men Over and Over to See If All Are Safe, Before Leaving The Boat

Fire of unknown origin burned the steamer Montana, belonging to C. W. Ketcher of Detroit, to the water's edge early Monday morning and it

STR FLINT BURNED ALSO ON HOLIDAY

The steamer Montana went to its fate on Labor Day. The last vessel burning off Alpena also was lost on a holiday.

That was the steamer Oscar T. Flint which was burned on Thanksgiving Day, 1909, six miles due east of the mouth of the river, all aboard escaping safely. The wreck was a menace to navigation until it was removed by the government the following year. It is hardly likely the burned Montana will prove a menace to navigation.

Thunder Bay Sanctuary Research Collection

The Death's Door Passage

An area of Lake Michigan was the site of so many shipwrecks that it had a nickname. This area, off the tip of Wisconsin's Door County, became known as "Death's Door."

Death's Door is the **strait** between Door County Peninsula and the islands not far to the northwest. The name Death's Door comes from the French name, ***Porte des Morts***. Some

---

strait (strayt): a narrow passage connecting two bodies of water
Porte des Morts: port de mor

University of Wisconsin Cartography Laboratory

The coast along Death's Door is treacherous!
Wikimedia Commons

people believe the strait got its name after a large Indian war party was destroyed there in a sudden storm. Early French and American travelers heard and repeated this story about "a hundred Indians dashed against these rocks and killed in a single storm." Some think that French fur traders spread this story to keep others from coming to the area. Due to its strong currents, fierce winds, and rocky shores, Death's Door is definitely known as a killer of ships. Lighthouses built on Plum Island (in 1848 and 1896) and Pilot Island (in 1850) helped, but hundreds of vessels have been lost or damaged in the Death's Door area.

One cold October night in 1891, the schooner *Forest* entered the Death's Door passage. A **gale** struck and drove the ship onto the reef at Pilot Island. The next day, the crew rowed to shore and the safety of the lighthouse.

The following fall, two more schooners—the *J. E. Gilmore* and the *A. P. Nichols*—wrecked at the same spot less than two weeks apart. On October 17, the *Gilmore* entered the passage at Death's Door in heavy, shifting winds and was blown onto the reef. The crew waited out the storm on board. On October 28, fierce winds and blinding snow struck the *Nichols*, tore apart her rigging, and drove her onto the rocks near the shipwrecked *Gilmore* and *Forest*. In a dangerous rescue, lighthouse keeper Martin Knudson and his lighthouse crew helped the sailors leap from the rolling *Nichols* onto the icy deck of the wrecked *Forest* to reach Pilot Island. Because of the bravery of the lifesaving crew, not one person was lost!

"Captain Santa" and the Christmas Tree Ship

During the 1800s, Chicago was one of the busiest shipping ports in the world. In 1875, nearly twenty-one thousand vessels passed through Chicago's harbor. Great Lakes ships carried nearly every commodity that passed through the bustling city—even Christmas trees!

---

gale: a strong storm with high winds

Herman **Schuenemann** had spent many years as a ship captain
on the Great Lakes. Beginning in 1890, each November, for the final
voyage of the season, he would load up the ship with evergreens
from Michigan and bring them to Chicago. He would dock along the
Chicago River and turn his ship into a floating Christmas tree lot!
It was said that the Christmas season had not begun until Captain
Schuenemann arrived with his ship at Clark Street dock, hoisted a
decorated tree up the mast, and strung electric lights throughout the
rigging. The captain treated his customers kindly and was generous
to those who didn't have a lot of money. His practice of giving
away many of his trees to churches and to the needy families of the
Chicago earned him the nickname "Captain Santa."

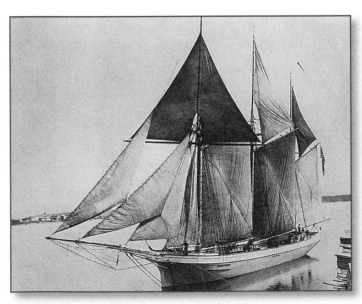

The *Rouse Simmons* was a beautiful schooner.
Thunder Bay Sanctuary Research Collection

The *Rouse Simmons*, docked in Chicago, was known as
the "Christmas Tree Ship."
Thunder Bay Sanctuary Research Collection

Schuenemann: **shoo** nuh muhn

Late in the afternoon of November 22, 1912, the temperature was falling and the winds were increasing as a snowstorm drew near. Captain Schuenemann's schooner, the *Rouse Simmons*, a three-masted sailing ship, left Thompson, Michigan, fully loaded with evergreens on her final voyage of the 1912 season. Before their departure, the kind-hearted Schuenemann invited aboard an unknown number of lumberjacks to catch a ride back to Chicago to spend the holidays with friends and family. But Captain Schuenemann, the *Rouse Simmons*, and her estimated sixteen crew members and passengers never arrived at Chicago. The schooner was lost with all hands somewhere on the lake.

Christmas trees washed up along the coastline for years to follow, and in 1923 the captain's wallet came up in a fisherman's net near Two Rivers, Wisconsin, but the location of the *Rouse Simmons* wreck remained a mystery for fifty-nine years. It was not until a Milwaukee diver discovered the vessel's remains in 165 feet of water twelve miles northeast of Two Rivers that the story began to unravel. The discovery solved the mystery of where the *Rouse Simmons* sank—but it may never be known for certain what transpired during the *Rouse Simmons*' final moments.

Wreck of the Rouse Simmons

Thompson

Michigan

Lake Michigan

N W E S

Wisconsin

Two Rivers — *Rouse Simmons*

0   25   50 Miles
0   25   50 Kilometers

University of Wisconsin Cartography Laboratory

A Superior Shipwreck: The Sinking of the *Lucerne*

Lake Superior is the largest and deepest of the Great Lakes, and its waters are icy cold, even in summer. Fall is the season for "**nor'easters**," storms with strong winds and heavy rain or snow. In November 1886, the schooner *Lucerne* loaded a cargo of iron ore at Ashland for the last trip of the season. The crew did not know that a terrible snowstorm would soon sweep across Lake Superior. The vessel was far from shelter when the storm hit. Struggling in the rough seas, with the wind and snow blowing fiercely, the *Lucerne* turned back for the safety of **Chequamegon** Bay.

As the *Lucerne* sailed through the blinding snowstorm, the crew probably did not know exactly where they were. Afraid of running aground, the captain dropped anchor in order to ride out the storm. At some point, the windlass, which controlled the anchor, stopped working. Icy water gushing over the decks may have frozen the windlass. Unable to control the anchor, the crew could not keep the *Lucerne* from being pushed backwards. An iron bar wedged into the windlass appears to have been a sailor's unsuccessful effort to repair it and stop the *Lucerne* from being pushed aground by the storm.

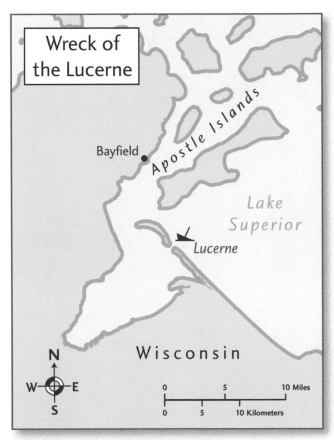

University of Wisconsin Cartography Laboratory

---

nor'easter: short for "northeaster"
Lucerne: loo **surn**
Chequamegon: shuh **wah** muh guhn

The *Lucerne,* docked next to a larger vessel
Thunder Bay Sanctuary Research Collection

The storm continued for two days. A lighthouse keeper spotted the ship off Long Island, only a few miles from the entrance to Chequamegon Bay. He saw only the *Lucerne*'s masts above water. Three men had climbed up the masts to escape Lake Superior's freezing waters. They were discovered tied to the rigging, covered with almost six inches of ice. There were no survivors.

For nearly one hundred years, the sinking of the *Lucerne* remained a mystery. Because there were no survivors, no one was left to tell the story. However, using various methods and equipment, underwater archaeologists were able to piece together the story of the *Lucerne*'s last days afloat. The wreck is a popular site for divers. It sits in the sandy lake floor off Long Island, near Ashland, Wisconsin. The top of the ship's bow, or front section, is fifteen feet below the water's surface. The ship's hull and part of the deck are still mostly **intact**. Pieces of the iron ore the ship was carrying at the time it sank are scattered in the sandy lake bottom around the wreck. If you want to learn more about this shipwreck, you can visit the *Lucerne* exhibit at Lake Superior Maritime Visitors Center in Duluth, Minnesota. It has many objects recovered from the wreck as well as a **reconstruction** of part of the ship.

intact: not broken or damaged
reconstruction: something rebuilt to look like the original

These are only a few examples of shipwrecks in places near Michigan and Wisconsin. There are many more shipwrecks with stories to tell. In the next chapter, you will learn how shipwrecks are discovered and how underwater archaeologists piece together the stories of shipwrecks to tell us more about ourselves and our history in the Great Lakes region.

An underwater diver checks the windlass of the wrecked *Lucerne*.
Photo by Tamara Thomsen,
Wisconsin Historical Society

9

Exploring Shipwrecks

Underwater archaeologists explore the wreck of the *Iris*, a schooner that ran aground in Jackson Harbor on Washington Island, just above Death's Door Passage, in March of 1913.
Photo by Tamara Thomsen, Wisconsin Historical Society

The Great Lakes can be very dangerous for the men and women who work upon their waters. Did you know there are probably over ten thousand shipwrecks in the Great Lakes? Each one is a museum waiting to be explored.

You have learned about our Great Lakes history from canoes to giant bulk freighters, but did you ever wonder how we know all this information about the past? Much of it comes from historical **documents** such as journals, newspapers, or letters written by people who actually lived at the time. But not enough written documents exist to tell us everything that we want to know about the past. Shipwrecks are a great source for learning more about our history.

In this chapter, you will explore the world of **underwater archaeology**. You will find the answers to many questions including: How are shipwrecks found? How do we study shipwrecks? Why did ships sink and what do they really tell us about our past? How do we preserve shipwrecks and their **artifacts**? Why is **preservation** so important?

---

documents: written information from a specific time
underwater archaeology: the study of shipwrecks and other underwater sites
artifacts: objects from the past that were made or used by people
preservation (pre zur **vay** shuhn): keeping something from being damaged or destroyed

Shipwrecks, Shipwrecks Everywhere

Shipwrecks are really time capsules. Archaeologists know that if a ship sank in 1859, everything on board came from 1859 or earlier. They can use the clothing, eating utensils, tools, navigational instruments, cargo, and personal items found on a shipwreck, and the ship itself, to understand how people lived and worked. Shipwrecks tell us what people did at a very specific time. Underwater archaeologists **interpret** sunken artifacts. They tell us how the ships were built and even why they sank.

Once it has come to rest on the bottom of a lake or river, a shipwreck often remains protected by the water that hides it. The cold, fresh water of the Great Lakes preserves materials much better than if the wreck happened on land or in salty ocean water. This explains why Great Lakes shipwrecks are considered some of the best preserved in the world. In some special cases, underwater archaeologists can find nearly everything that was aboard a ship when it sailed.

There are thousands of shipwrecks in the Great Lakes and over two hundred just around Thunder Bay in Lake Huron. Remember that many thousands of ships sailed in and out of ports all across the Great Lakes. Some older, rundown ships were abandoned in shallow water or even set on fire on purpose. By looking at one Great Lakes shipwreck, we will discover its story through underwater archaeology.

Did You Know?

Beneath the lakes and rivers lie not just shipwrecks but also thousands of other archaeological sites. In Chapter 2, you learned that the Great Lakes were formed by the movement of glaciers. You also learned that the Great Lakes and its region changed over time because of weather. As the lakes rose, they covered land where people once lived. Archaeologists have found the remains of fur trading posts, lumber mills, quarries, and other structures underwater. They have also found objects such as ice harvesting tools and early Indian fishing gear. Underwater archaeologists study these artifacts to learn more about our past.

---

interpret: to explain the meaning of something

Divers take careful measurements of an underwater shipwreck.
NOAA, Thunder Bay National Marine Sanctuary

The Sinking of the *Cornelia B. Windiate*

In November 1875, the schooner *Cornelia B. **Windiate*** left Milwaukee, Wisconsin, for its last trip of the season. The ship was filled to the brim with grain, more than she could carry safely. The crew did not know that a terrible winter storm would soon sweep across Lakes Michigan and Huron. The vessel was far from shelter when the storm hit. Struggling through the rough seas, strong winds, and heavy snow, the *Windiate* made it much farther than anyone could have expected before it sank.

As the *Windiate* sailed through the blinding snowstorm, the crew probably did not know exactly where they were. Spray crashing onto the rigging and icy water gushing over the decks may have coated

Windiate: win dee uht

The *Cornelia B. Windiate*
Painting by Robert McGreevey, NOAA, Thunder Bay National Marine Sanctuary

the ship with thick layers of ice. The thick ice weighed the ship down.
The combination of the ice on the decks and rigging and the heavy
cargo below would have been too much for the *Windiate*. Eventually
the waves would have **swamped** the *Windiate*, sinking her along
with a crew of nine men. While the ice that built up on the decks
probably helped sink the ship, it also played an important role in its
preservation. **Encased** in ice, the *Windiate* would have been slightly
buoyant, like an ice cube floating in a glass of water. The ice would
have slowly melted in the water, bringing the ship to rest gently on
the bottom of the lake without damaging it.

---

swamped: sunk
encased: completely covered

The deck of the *Windiate*
Photo by Rob Maxon

For just over one hundred years, the sinking of the *Windiate* remained a mystery. Because there were no survivors, no one was left to tell the story. The site of the shipwreck wasn't discovered for many years. However, underwater archaeologists were able to piece together the story of the *Windiate*'s last days afloat. Let's find out exactly how they did it.

Tamara Thomsen and Keith Meverden, underwater archeologists from the Wisconsin Historical Society, use a historic map to locate a shipwreck site.
Photo Courtesy of Tamara Thomsen, Wisconsin Historical Society

Searching for Shipwrecks

Sometimes fishermen accidentally discover shipwrecks. Sometimes **scuba divers** search for unknown shipwrecks for the excitement of discovery and to have more sites to explore. But how do underwater archaeologists discover shipwrecks? The search begins in the library, where archaeologists conduct historical research. This first step is often the most important, since archaeologists find clues about shipwrecks in the journals of sailors, the **logs** of lighthouse keepers, maps, newspaper articles, and other records.

scuba divers: divers who use special gear for breathing underwater
logs: daily, sometimes hourly, written accounts of events

Archaeologists used journals and newspaper accounts to find out details about the *Windiate*'s last voyage. They learned where the ship was headed, what cargo it was carrying, and what the weather was like on Lake Huron the day that it sank. This information helped them connect what they knew about the *Windiate* to a shipwreck discovered by **recreational** divers off of **Presque Isle,** Michigan in 1986.

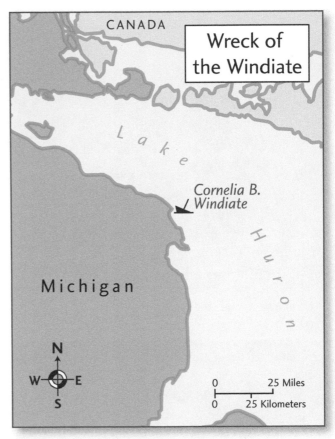

University of Wisconsin Cartography Laboratory

Often, underwater archaeologists search for shipwrecks themselves. Sometimes archaeologists are looking for a particular wreck. In other cases they are trying to find all of the wrecks in an area. Depending on the size of the search area and how deep and clear the water is, archaeologists look for shipwrecks in several ways. One way is a **visual** search. A visual search works best in shallow water where it is easy to see the bottom. Archaeologists can do visual searches from an airplane, by looking over the side of a boat, or by swimming or being towed across an area by a boat, using scuba equipment and snorkels.

If the search area is very large or in deep water where it is difficult to see, electronic equipment can help locate shipwrecks. Archaeologists control this equipment from a boat.

---

recreational: doing something just for fun
Presque Isle: presk **eel**
visual (**vizh** oo uhl): by sight

A diver investigates the *McCool*.
Photo by Tamara Thomsen, Wisconsin Historical Society

The *McCool* was lost in shallow water off of Bayfield, Wisconsin, in 1958.
Photo by Tamara Thomsen, Wisconsin Historical Society

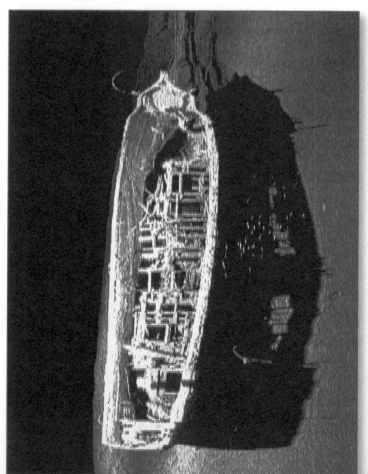

Sonar images, like this one of the *Rouse Simmons*, help underwater archaeologists figure out why ships sank.
Courtesy of VideoRay

For example, an underwater metal detector called a **magnetometer** picks up signals from metal parts on a shipwreck. The magnetometer gives off a signal when it passes over a metal object and records these targets on a computer. Divers later return and investigate these "targets" to see if the metal object that set off the signal is actually part of a shipwreck.

Another piece of equipment, called **sonar**, also can detect shipwrecks. Sonar equipment uses sound waves that bounce off the lake or river bottom. These sound waves return a signal to the ship. A computer records these signals and produces an image of the lake bottom. Just as they do with the magnetometer, archaeologists identify "targets." Then divers go underwater to inspect the area.

Documenting Shipwrecks

Once archaeologists locate a shipwreck, they study it in great detail. They **document** everything they find. Their records include **observations**, measurements, and artifacts. Documenting a shipwreck is almost like writing a history book. If the shipwreck is not examined properly or artifacts are removed without recording them, it is like tearing pages from the book—pages that will be lost forever.

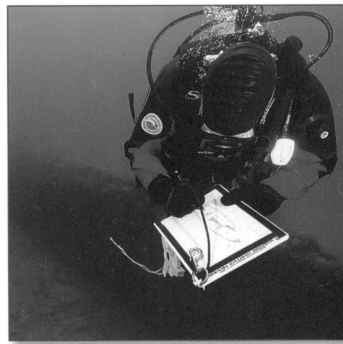

This diver takes careful notes—in pencil—on his slate.
NOAA, Thunder Bay National Marine Sanctuary

magnetometer: mag nuh **tah** muh tur
sonar (**soh** nahr): short for **so**und **na**vigation **a**nd **r**anging
document: record
observations: things you notice by watching carefully

The **site plan** of the *Windiate* is exact down to the last detail.
NOAA, Thunder Bay National Marine Sanctuary

Sometimes archaeologists go underwater and map the entire shipwreck exactly as it appears. They take measurements and make detailed drawings on waterproof paper using an ordinary pencil. Underwater archaeologists often divide a shipwreck into small sections. Each archaeologist records the ship parts and artifacts in his or her area. These drawings, along with underwater video and photographs, are later pieced together on shore to form a complete picture of the shipwreck, much like putting together a jigsaw puzzle.

This process of carefully mapping a shipwreck creates a site plan. Site plans help archaeologists see how the whole site looks. They can tell exactly where parts of the ship are in relation to other things on board and around the site. Archaeologists can also see from site plans how the ship was built. Sometimes, they can even see how or why the ship sank. Site plans are difficult to create because sometimes the wreck is very large, scattered in many pieces, or covered with marine life like **zebra mussels**.

site plan: a carefully measured drawing that archaeologists make of a shipwreck and the artifacts on or around it
zebra mussels: small shellfish with zig-zag markings on their shells

A diver checks out the zebra mussels on the inside of the *Grecian*.
NOAA, Thunder Bay National Marine Sanctuary

A photomosaic of the *Windiate*
NOAA, Thunder Bay National Marine Sanctuary

Sketches also help experts determine the reasons ships sank. This is a sketch of the *Windiate* on the lake floor.
NOAA, Thunder Bay National Marine Sanctuary

Archaeologists can also piece together images from photographs and video taken by divers. This process creates a photomosaic of the wreck site. A photomosaic is not measured, but it gives archaeologists a look at the shipwreck just as it is underwater. Because visibility can be very poor underwater and wrecks are often very large, taking many small pictures of a shipwreck and piecing them together is a great way to see all of the details of the whole wreck at once.

During the dives to gather information about the *Windiate*, archaeologists discovered several things about the shipwreck. First, they found that the shipwreck was surprisingly intact. There were no holes in the hull. Holes would have been clues that the ship ran aground or was involved in a collision. The *Windiate* crew's lifeboat was also sitting right next to the ship. The lifeboat's location told the archaeologists the crew hadn't tried to leave the ship as it was sinking. This fact **suggests** that the weather must have been so rough that the crew would not have been able to survive in their tiny rowboat. Divers also found the

suggests: gives hints

Windiate's cargo of grain. The grain was still in the cargo holds, filled right up to the level of the deck. This proved that the ship had been overloaded on its final voyage.

Because archaeologists were able to study the *Windiate*'s artifacts, the story of what happened so many years ago was also preserved. If artifacts had been missing, the fate of the sailors would have remained a mystery. The team was able to tell a story that would have otherwise gone untold because they combined historical library research and archaeological investigation.

Conserving Shipwrecks

As a rule, archaeologists do not remove artifacts from shipwrecks for souvenirs. Shipwreck divers are told to "take only pictures and leave only bubbles." Sometimes, however, they may want to remove a few special artifacts for study or to place in a museum for the public to see. Because these artifacts have been wet for many years, they must first be **conserved**. Conservation is expensive and takes a lot of time. That is why archaeologists remove only what they need for research or public education.

Conserving artifacts is one way to share them with the public. But underwater archaeologists have other options. Sometimes, they leave artifacts in place as "underwater museums." Archaeologists take only information, such as notes and photos. Then they write books or reports or create websites to share their research with others.

---

conserved: treated to prevent decay

This is the **safe** from the *Pewabic,* before and after it was conserved.
NOAA, Thunder Bay National Marine Sanctuary

One of the ways we can protect the artifacts on shipwrecks and shipwrecks themselves is by passing laws that make it illegal for anyone to remove artifacts or damage shipwrecks. In some areas, laws are already in place. In 1981, the state of Michigan recognized the importance of the shipwrecks in Thunder Bay. The state created what is called an underwater **preserve**. The underwater preserve protects the wrecks that lay in it.

In 2000, the US government recognized the importance of the shipwrecks in Thunder Bay by creating Thunder Bay National Marine Sanctuary and Underwater Preserve as the thirteenth

safe: a box with a lock for storing money or valuables
preserve: protected place

national marine sanctuary or underwater park. The Thunder Bay National Marine Sanctuary was the first national marine sanctuary in fresh water. Both the state and federal governments have been working together to protect the nearly two hundred shipwrecks in Thunder Bay ever since.

What is a National Marine Sanctuary?

What does it mean that Thunder Bay became a national marine sanctuary in 2000? Why does this help protect the shipwrecks of Thunder Bay? In 1972, the US government created a law to protect special areas of water in the United States by naming them national marine sanctuaries. Being named a national marine sanctuary means that a place is special and important to the country, a place that needs to be protected and preserved for future generations of Americans. Thunder Bay is the only national marine sanctuary in the Great Lakes region.

It takes a lot of work to protect the resources found inside a national marine sanctuary. The people working at the sanctuary in Thunder Bay protect and preserve the wrecks on the bottom of the lake, study and document those shipwrecks, learn how they fit into the history of the Great Lakes region, and teach people about the shipwrecks of Thunder Bay.

A **mooring buoy**
NOAA, Thunder Bay National Marine Sanctuary

---

mooring buoy (**boo** ee): floating marker

At the Great Lakes Maritime Heritage Center, people learn about shipwrecks in Thunder Bay.

NOAA, Thunder Bay National Marine Sanctuary

The sanctuary also works to help divers visit shipwrecks more easily and to understand more about the shipwrecks that they visit. It provides divers and boaters with the locations of many of the shipwrecks in and around Thunder Bay. The sanctuary also puts mooring buoys in the water to show divers and boaters where shipwrecks are located. Mooring buoys also provide a place to tie up a boat without having to drop an anchor, which could land on a shipwreck and damage it.

But what about people who live far away from Thunder Bay or who can't dive underwater to visit shipwrecks in person? The Thunder Bay National Marine Sanctuary also has a visitor's center in Alpena, Michigan. The Great Lakes Maritime Heritage Center is a museum where thousands of people come every year to learn about the Great Lakes and the shipwrecks of Thunder Bay.

Past, Present, and Future

Studying maritime history can help us understand how people in the Great Lakes region lived and worked. It can also tell us how they used one of their greatest natural resources—water.

But preserving the past is as important as studying the past. We need to look after our resources. We do not want to lose or destroy our waterways—even by accident. Much of the history of the Great Lakes states has taken place along these waterways, and this history is important to our understanding of North America. We need to protect not only the lakes and rivers, but also the shipwrecks, lighthouses, and other landmarks that make the Great Lakes region special.

Abandoned Shipwreck Act of 1988

Shipwrecks are an important cultural resource to many different people, from divers to historians to students like you. The Abandoned Shipwreck Act was signed into law in 1988 to make sure that shipwrecks are available to everyone and not just a few people. This law makes individual states the owners of historic shipwrecks. And if a state owns a shipwreck, it is against the law to damage the wreck or remove artifacts from it. Each state works together with partners, such as underwater archaeologists, to protect historic shipwrecks. Protection can include providing mooring buoys at wreck sites or information to the public at museums.

Time Line

500 million years ago	The Great Lakes region is underwater.
15,000 years ago	Glaciers begin to create lakes on the North American continent.
14,000–6,000 BCE	The Great Lakes are shaped by glaciers.
10,000 BCE	The first people arrive in the region.
1500s and 1600s	Exploration of the Americas by Europeans begins.
1620	The first British colony is started in the Americas.
1634	Jean Nicolet arrives at Red Banks near Green Bay.
1679	The first ship to sail the upper Great Lakes, the *Griffon*, disappears.
1755	The *Oswego*, the first British ship to sail the Great Lakes, is built.
1756–1763	French and Indian War
1760	The British take over all of the land that the French had claimed in Canada and the Great Lakes region.
1775–1783	American Revolution

1783   The Great Lakes are established as border between the United States and British-controlled Canada.

1812–1815   War of 1812

1813   Congress passes a law allowing black men who had been born in the United States to join the military.

On August 9, the *Hamilton* and *Scourge* sink in Lake Ontario during a sudden squall.

1817   Construction begins on the Erie Canal.

1818   The first two lighthouses are built on the Great Lakes in Buffalo, New York, and Erie, Pennsylvania.

1825   The Eric Canal opens.

Wisconsin tribes sign a treaty with the US government at Prairie du Chien, and give up their land to white settlers.

1829   The Welland Canal opens.

1837   Michigan becomes a state.

1848   Wisconsin becomes a state.

1849   The *New Orleans* becomes the first known shipwreck in Lake Huron's treacherous Thunder Bay.

1855   The Soo Locks are built at Sault Sainte Marie.

1865 — The *Pewabic* and *Meteor* collide off Thunder Bay Island.

1869 — The *R.J. Hackett* becomes the first bulk freighter on the Great Lakes.

1870 — The number of sailing vessels on the Great Lakes peaks.

1875 — Nearly 21,000 vessels pass through Chicago's harbor.

The *Cornelia B. Windiate* sinks in snowstorm.

1886 — The *Lucerne* wrecks in a snowstorm sweeping Lake Superior.

1891 — The *Forest* wrecks in Death's Door passage at the tip of Door Peninsula in Wisconsin.

1892 — Two more schooners—the *J.E. Gilmore* and the *A.P. Nichols*—wreck in the same passage of Death's Door.

1906 — Steel freighters on the Great Lakes reach over 600 feet.

1912 — The *Rouse Simmons*, also known as the "Christmas Tree Ship," sinks during a snowstorm in Lake Michigan.

1913 — The "Great Storm of 1913" sinks eight ships and kills over two hundred sailors on Lake Huron.

1914   The *Montana* burns and sinks in Thunder Bay, Michigan.

1971   The *Rouse Simmons* wreckage is discovered near Two Rivers, Wisconsin.

1972   The US government passes a law to protect special areas of water called national marine sanctuaries.

1973   The *Hamilton* and *Scourge* wreckages are discovered near St. Catherines, Ontario, in Lake Ontario.

1976   The *Cornelia B. Windiate* is discovered by recreational divers in Lake Huron near Rogers City, Michigan.

1981   The State of Michigan creates an underwater preserve at Thunder Bay.

1988   The US government passes the Abandoned Shipwreck Act to protect shipwrecks in state waters.

1996   A piece of the Lake Mary Canoe, built 2,000 years ago, is discovered in Kenosha, Wisconsin.

2000   The US government recognizes Thunder Bay as a National Marine Sanctuary and Underwater Preserve.

To Learn More

Books

Ayer, Eleanor. *Our Great Rivers and Waterways.* I Know America Series. Brookfield, CT: Millbrook, 1994.

Berton, Pierre. *Battle of Lake Erie: Battles of the War of 1812.* Toronto: McClelland & Stewart Limited, 1994.

Butts, Ed. *Shipwrecks, Monsters, and Mysteries of the Great Lakes.* Ontario: Tundra Books, 2011.

Ernst, Kathleen. *Trouble at Fort La Pointe.* Middleton, WI: Pleasant Company, 2000.

Halsey, John R. and Wayne R. Lusardi. *Beneath the Inland Seas, Michigan's Underwater Archaeological Heritage.* Ann Arbor: Michigan Dept. of History, Arts, and Libraries, 2008.

Hiscock, Bruce. *The Big Rivers: The Missouri, the Mississippi, and the Ohio.* New York: Atheneum Books for Young Readers, 1997.

House, Katherine L. *Lighthouses for Kids: History, Science, and More with 21 Activities.* Chicago, Chicago Press Review, 2008.

Karamanski, Theodore J. *Schooner Passage: Sailing Ships and the Lake Michigan Frontier.* Detroit: Wayne State University Press, 2000.

Kendall, Martha E. *The Erie Canal.* Des Moines: National Geographic Children's Books, 2008.

Leow, Patty. *Native People of Wisconsin.* Madison: Wisconsin Historical Society Press, 2003.

Malone, Bobbie and Kori Oberle. *Wisconsin: Our State, Our Story.* Madison: Wisconsin Historical Society Press, 2008.

Varhola, Michael J. *Shipwrecks and Lost Treasures: Great Lakes Legends and Lore, Pirates and More.* Guilford, CT: Globe Pequot Press, 2007.

Web Sites

Columbia University Interactive Maritime Timeline: http://beatl.barnard.columbia.edu/beatldb/maritimedb/admin/searchTimeline.asp

Death's Door Shipwrecks, University of Wisconsin Sea Grant: www.wisconsinshipwrecks.org/tools_deathsdoor.cfm

Door County Lighthouses: www.lighthousefriends.com/door.html

EPA Wetlands: http://water.epa.gov/type/wetlands/

Michigan DNR / Michigan Historical Museum: First People: www.hal.state.mi.us/mhc/firstpeople/

Michigan Underwater Preserves: www.michiganpreserves.org

The Great Lakes Information Network (GLIN): www.great-lakes.net/teach

Great Lakes Lighthouse Keepers Association: www.gllka.com

NOAA Great Lakes Quick Facts: www.glerl.noaa.gov/pr/ourlakes/lakes.html#superior

Thunder Bay National Marine Sanctuary: Thunder Bay History: http://thunderbay.noaa.gov

USGS Education Resources: http://water.usgs.gov/education.html

Wisconsin Historical Society Underwater Archeology:
www.wisconsinhistory.org/shipwrecks/learn/

Wisconsin's Maritime Trails: www.maritimetrails.org

For more resources about maritime history on the Great Lakes, please refer to the Great Ships on the Great Lakes Teachers' Guide.

Places to Visit

40 Mile Point Lighthouse Park
US 23 North
Rogers City, MI 49779
www.40milepointlighthouse.org

Apostle Islands National Lakeshore
415 Washington Ave.
Bayfield, WI 54814
www.nps.gov/apis/planyourvisit/directions.htm

Bayfield Maritime Museum
131 S. 1st St.
Bayfield, WI 54814
www.bayfieldmaritimemuseum.org

Chippewa Moraine Ice Age Interpretive Center
13394 County Hwy. M
New Auburn, WI 54757
http://dnr.wi.gov/org/land/parks/specific/
chipmoraine/center.html

Door County Maritime Museum
120 N. Madison Ave.
Sturgeon Bay, WI 54235
www.dcmm.org

Dossin Great Lakes Museum
100 Strand Drive, Belle Isle
Detroit, MI 48207
www.detroithistorical.org

Great Lakes Maritime Heritage Center
Thunder Bay National Marine Sanctuary
500 W. Fletcher St.
Alpena, MI 49707
http://thunderbay.noaa.gov

Erie Maritime Museum and Homeport Flagship
Niagara
150 East Front Street
Erie, PA 16507
www.eriemaritimemuseum.org

Great Lakes Naval Museum
610 Farragut Ave., Building 42
Great Lakes, IL 60888
www.history.navy.mil/museums/greatlakes/
index.htm

Great Lakes Shipwreck Museum–White Fish
Point
18335 N. Whitefish Point Road
Paradise, MI 49768
www.shipwreckmuseum.com/grouptours

Interstate Park Ice Age Interpretive Center
Hwy 35
St. Croix Falls, WI 54024
http://dnr.wi.gov/topic/parks/name/interstate/

Madeline Island Museum
226 Colonel Woods Ave.
La Pointe, WI 54850
madelineislandmuseum.wisconsinhistory.org

The Michigan Historical Museum
702 W. Kalamazoo St.
Lansing, MI 48915
www.michigan.gov/museum

Michigan Maritime Museum
260 Dyckman Ave.
South Haven, MI 49090
www.michiganmaritimemuseum.org

The Museum of Ojibwa Culture
566 N. State St.
St. Ignace, MI 49781

National Museum of the Great Lakes
1701 Front Street
Toledo, OH 43605
nmgl.org

Old Mackinac Point Lighthouse
526 N. Huron Ave.
Mackinaw City, MI 49701

Soo Locks Park and Visitor Center
1808 Ashmun St.
Sault Ste. Marie, MI 49783

SS *Meteor* Maritime Museum
300 Marina Dr.
Superior, WI 54880

Thunder Bay National Marine Sanctuary
See Great Lakes Maritime Heritage Center

Wisconsin Maritime Museum
75 Maritime Dr.
Manitowoc, WI 54220
www.wisconsinmaritime.org

For more places to visit and learn about maritime history on the Great Lakes, please refer to the Great Ships on the Great Lakes *Teachers' Guide.*

About the Authors

Catherine M. Green is an underwater archaeologist specializing in outreach and education programs with Thunder Bay National Marine Sanctuary. Cathy combines her background in nautical archaeology with her experience teaching in shipboard education programs to bring the maritime heritage resources of the sanctuary to a wide audience.

Courtesy of Catherine M. Green

Courtesy of Jefferson J. Gray

Jefferson J. Gray has served as the superintendent of the Thunder Bay National Marine Sanctuary in Alpena, Michigan, since 2002. The sanctuary protects the Great Lakes and their rich maritime history through research, education, and resource protection so this and future generations can enjoy these underwater treasures.

Photo by Joe Heiman

As former director of the Office of School Services at the Wisconsin Historical Society, **Bobbie Malone** wrote and edited many books for classrooms, including the fourth grade textbook, *Wisconsin: Our State, Our Story*; the New Badger History series; and the Badger Biographies series. Now she consults with school districts and museums and is busily working on a biography of author-illustrator Lois Lenski.

Index

This index points you to the pages where you can read about persons, places, and ideas. If you do not find the word you are looking for, try to think of another word that means about the same thing.

When you see a page number in **bold** it means there is a picture on that page.

A

A. P. Nichols, 98

Abandoned Shipwreck Act (1988), 119

African Americans
    sailors, 40
    ship cooks, 73

Alpena wetlands, Michigan, **13**

Apostle Islands National Lakeshore, 11

archaeological sites, under the Great Lakes, 105

archaeologists, underwater, **104**, **106, 108, 110, 111, 113**
    and *Cornelia B. Windiate*, 109, 114–115
    documenting shipwrecks, 111–112, 114–115
    searching for shipwrecks, 108–109, 111
    and shipwreck conservation, 115–117
    tools used to find shipwrecks, 109, 111

B

Banai, Edward Benton, 6

Battle of Lake Erie (1813), **37, 38**

Bayfield caves, Wisconsin, **5**

birchbark canoes, 19–20, **19, 20**, 22

"Blow the Man Down" (song), 74

bogs. *See* wetlands

Braddock, Edward, 33

breakwaters, 57

brigs. *See* ships

British people
    as fur traders, 31–32
    as settlers, 31–32
    and War of 1812, 36–39
    See also Europeans; settlers

Bruce Peninsula, Canada, 10

bulk freighters. *See* freighters

C

Canada, 35, **35**

canalers, 60

canals
    Erie Canal, 46–48, **47, 48**, 55
    and locks, 58–60, **58**
    map of, **58**
    Welland Canal, 58–60

cannons, 39, **39**

canoes
    birchbark, 19–20, **19, 20**, 22
    dugout, 18–19, **18**
    of French fur traders, 23–24, **23**
    Montreal Canoe, 23, **24**
    Nord Canoe, 24, **25**
    used in wild rice harvests, **17**

carronades, 39, **41**

Charles H. Bradley, **63**

Chicago, Illinois, 49, **49**

Christians, 6

Christmas Tree Ship (*Rouse Simmons*), 98–100, **99**

City of Racine, **64**

City of Toledo, 78

Cleveland, Ohio, 48, **49**

conservation, 115–117

cooks, 73

Cornelia B. Windiate, 106–108, **107**, **108**, **109**, 112, 113, 114–115, **114**

creation stories, 6

D

Death's Door Passage, 96–98, **97**

Detroit, Michigan, 49, **49**, 51

Detroit River, **3**

divers. *See* scuba divers

Door County, Wisconsin, 10, 75, 96–98

dugout canoes, 18–19, **18**

Duluth, Minnesota, 59

E

Edmund Fitzgerald, 66, **66**

Erie Canal, **47**, **48**
  building of, 46–48
  and shipping boom, 55

Erie people, 25

Europeans
  arrival of, to Great Lakes region, 21–22, **22**, 30–31
  and naming of Great Lakes, 25
  as settlers, 45–46
  trading with Natives, 22
  See also British people; French people

F

Fedora, **84**

figureheads, 42, **42**

floods, 5

foghorns, 78

Forest, 98

Fort William, **23**

forts, 30, 32

Francis Hinton, **77**

freighters
  Edmund Fitzgerald, 66, **66**
  in Green Bay Harbor, Wisconsin, **3**
  Isaac M. Scott, 89–90, **89**
  loading and unloading cargo for, 68–69, **68**, **69**
  modern, 67–69
  Nyanza, **73**
  R. J. Hackett, **65**
  steel, **65**, 66

French and Indian War, 33–34, **33**, 40

French people
  conflicts with British, 32
  as fur traders, 23–24, 28, 30
  as settlers, 32
  See also Europeans

Frontenac, 26

fur traders
  canoes of, 23–24, **23–24**
  as early explorers, 28, 30–31
  French and British conflicts, 32
  water routes of, **29**

G

geologists, 7

glaciers, 8–11, **9**, **10**

Great Eight states, 48–50, **49**

Great Lakes
  as border between US and Canada, 35, **35**, 43
  canals of, 43
  flow of, to Atlantic Ocean, 12
  formed by glaciers, 8–11, **10**
  and Great Eight states, **49**
  lighthouses in, **76**
  naming of, 25
  ships on, 56–57
  shorelines of, 10–11
  as travel route, 46
  warships as forbidden on, 43

Great Lakes Maritime Heritage Center, Alpena, Michigan, **118**

Great Lakes region
  Europeans' arrival to, 21–22, **22**, 30–31
  geographical history of, 7–9
  as land for pioneers, 36
  map of, **1**
  port cities of, 49, **49**, **51**, **52**
  shipping boom in, 55, 57
  St. Lawrence Seaway as route to, **21**
  waterways of, **11**

Great Storm of 1913, 89–90

Grecian, **113**

Green Bay Harbor, Wisconsin, **3**

Griffon, 26–27, **26**, **27**, 55

H

Hamilton, 41–42, **41**, **43**

history, maritime, 1

Hudson River, 46

Hulett shovel, **68**

I

ice, **4**

ice ages, 8

Illinois, 48–50

immigrants. *See* British people; Europeans; French people

Indiana, 48–50

Indians. *See* Native people

Iris, **104**

Iroquois people, 25

Isaac M. Scott, 89–90, **89**

J

J. E. Gilmore, 98

Jewish people, 6

K

kayaks, **3**

Kenosha, Wisconsin, **44**

L

La Salle, Robert de, 26–27, 55

Lake Erie
  naming of, 25
  settlement after War of 1812, 43
  and Welland Canal, 58
  See also Erie Canal

Lake Huron
  naming of, 25
  shipwrecks in, 86–96, 109
  and Soo Locks, 59

Lake Michigan
  naming of, 25
  shipwrecks in, 99–100, 104, 110, 113

Lake Ontario
  naming of, 25
  settlement after War of 1812, 43
  shipwrecks in, 27, 41–42
  and Welland Canal, 58–59

Lake Superior
  naming of, 25
  shipwrecks in, 84, 101–102
  and Soo Locks, 59

Lake Superior Maritime Visitors
  Center, Duluth, Minnesota, 102

Lawrence, 37–38, 40

libraries, 80

lifesaving stations, 77

Lighthouse Association, 80

lighthouse keepers
  Cecilia Persons, 82
  Derrick Simonson, 81
  Edith Morgan, 78
  Ella Luick, 81–82
  families of, 80–83
  Glenn Furst, 80
  jobs of, 78–79
  John Persons, 82
  Martin Knudson, 98
  Rachel Wolcott, 82

lighthouses
  in Death's Door Passage, 97–98
  defined, 77
  foghorns, 78
  lamps of, 78
  lenses, 79, **79**
  Marblehead Lighthouse, Ohio, 74, **75**
  origins of, 74–75
  and shipping industry, 83
  South Manitou Island
    Lighthouse, Michigan, **80**
  South Superior Entry
    Lighthouse, Wisconsin, 81
  Split Rock Lighthouse, Two
    Harbors, Minnesota, **79**
  Thunder Bay Island Lighthouse,
    Michigan, **82**

in western Great Lakes, **76**
  Wind Point Lighthouse, Racine,
    Wisconsin, **70**

lightships, 77, **77**

limestone quarry, **7**

locks, 58–60, **58**, **59**

long guns, 39, **39**, **41**

Lucerne, 101–103, **102**, **103**

M

Mackinac, Michigan, 49

Mackinaw, **83**

maps
  Cornelia B. Windiate shipwreck,
    109
  Death's Door Passage, **97**
  Erie Canal, **47**
  glaciers' impact on Great Lakes,
    10
  Great Eight, **49**
  Great Lakes region, **1**
  Griffon's journey, **27**
  lighthouses on the Great Lakes,
    76
  Lucerne shipwreck, **101**
  North America (1750), 31
  Rouse Simmons shipwreck, **99**
  shipbuilding locations (1850–
    1930), **61**
  sinking of *Hamilton* and
    Scourge, **43**
  Thunder Bay, Michigan, **87**
  US–Canada border, **35**
  water routes (1800s), **54**
  water routes during fur trade, **29**

Marblehead Lighthouse, Ohio, 3,
  74, **75**, 82

maritime history, 119

marshes. *See* wetlands

McCool, **110**

McDougall, Alexander, 66

Menominee River, **67**

Meteor (schooner), 93–94, **93**

Meteor (whaleback), **66**

Michigan
    lighthouses in, 75
    as one of the Great Eight states,
        48–50
    water routes to (1800s), **54**

Michigan Wetlands Restoration
    and Watershed Planning, 13

Milwaukee, Wisconsin, 49, **49**, **52**

Milwaukee River, **57**

Minnesota, 48–50

Mishomis Book, The (Banai), 6

missions, 28

Mohawk River, 46

Montana, **95**, 96

Montreal Canoe, 23, **24**

mooring buoys, **117**, 118

Myers, Ned, 42

N

national marine sanctuaries,
    116–118

Native people
    creation stories of, 6
    forced relocation of, 31, 50–51
    during French and Indian War,
        33
    and naming of Great Lakes, 25
    and smallpox, 31
    trading with Europeans, 22

trails of, 50

treaty at Prairie du Chien, **50**

waterways as transportation
    routes for, 16–17

wild rice harvests, 17

See also specific tribes

New Orleans, 90–92, **91**

New York, 48–50

Niagara, 38, **38**

Niagara Falls, **12**, 59

Nord Canoe, 24, **25**

Northwest Territory, 36, 38

Nyanza, **73**

O

Ohio, 48–50

Ojibwe people
    building canoes, **19**
    creation stories of, 6
    and naming of Great Lakes, 25

Oswego, 33, **33**

Ottawa, **71**

P

peninsulas, 10–11

Pennsylvania, 48–50

Perry, Oliver Hazard, 37–38, **37**

Persons, Cecilia, 82

Persons, John, 82

Peshtigo, **77**

Pewabic, 92–94, **93**, **94**, **116**

photomosaics, **94**, **113**, 114

Pictured Rocks National Lakeshore,
    Michigan, **5**, 10–11

pig boats, 66

Point Pelee National Park, 11

portage, 19, **19**

propellers, 62, 63

Q

quarries, **7**

R

R. J. Hackett, **65**

Revolutionary War, 34–35

Rouse Simmons, 99–100, **99**, **110**

S

sailing, dangers of, 70, 74–75

sailing rigs. *See* ships

sailors
    African Americans, 40, 73
    daily life of, 72–73
    food for, 73
    immigrants, 71
    schooner crew, **72**
    women, 73

Sault Sainte Marie, Michigan, 49,
    59

schooners, **57**, **71**
    canalers as, 60
    Cornelia B. Windiate, 106–108,
        107, **108**, **109**, **112**, **113**, 114–
        115, **114**
    Forest, 98
    Hamilton, 41
    J. E. Gilmore, 98
    Lucerne, 101–103, **102**, **103**
    Ottawa, **71**
    A. P. Nichols, 98
    replaced by steamships, 60

Rouse Simmons, 99–100, **99, 110**

Scourge, 41–42, **43**

compared to square-rigged
vessels, 55, **56**

Vega, **71**

during War of 1812, 41

Schuenemann, Herman, 99

Scourge, 41–42, **43**

scuba divers, **104, 106,** 108, **110,
111, 113**

sea shanties (songs), 73–74

settlers

changes to waterways by, 52

and Erie Canal, 46–48

move to Great Lakes region,
50–52

search for travel routes by, 46

See also British people;
Europeans; French people

shipbuilding

improvements in, 62–63

locations (1850–1930), **61**

shipping industry

boom in, 55, 57

and Erie Canal, 55

freighters, 65, **65**

and lighthouses, 83

loading and unloading cargo for,
68–69, **68, 69**

modern, 67–69

on steamships, 62

ships

canalers, 60

Charles H. Bradley, **63**

City of Racine, **64**

City of Toledo, 78

Edmund Fitzgerald, 66, **66**

figureheads of, **42**

Francis Hinton, 77

freighters, **3,** 65

during French and Indian War,
33, 40

Frontenac, 26

for Great Lakes compared to
oceans, 56–57

Grecian, **113**

Griffon, 26–27, **26,** 55

Hamilton, 41–42, **41**

Lawrence, 37–38, 40

lightships, **77**

Lucerne, **102**

Mackinaw, **83**

Meteor, 93–94, **93**

Niagara, **38**

Nyanza, **73**

Oswego, 33, **33**

Ottawa, **71**

Peshtigo, **77**

Rouse Simmons, **99**

schooners, 41, 55, **56, 57,** 60

schooners compared to square-
rigged, **56**

shipbuilding locations (1850–
1930), **61**

steamships, 60–61

steel compared to wood, 65

Vega, **71**

during War of 1812, 36–39

warships, 36–39, **39,** 41–43

shipwreck alley, 86–88

"Shipwreck Century" (1825–1925),
85–86

shipwrecks, **85, 106**

Abandoned Shipwreck Act
(1988), 119

as archaeological sites, 105

bad weather as cause of, 89

causes, 89, 95, 107, 90–91

conserving, 115–117

Cornelia B. Windiate, 106–108,
107, 108, 109, 112, 113, 114

crowded shipping lanes as cause
of, 92

documenting, 111–112, 114–115

Fedora, **84**

Grecian, **113**

figureheads of, 42

fire as cause of, 95

Frontenac, 27

Griffon, 27

Hamilton, 41–42

ice as cause of, 107

Iris, **104**

Isaac M. Scott, 89–90, **89**

Lucerne, 101–103, **103**

McCool, **110**

Meteor (schooner), 93–94, **93**

Montana, 96, **96**

New Orleans, 90–92

Pewabic, 92–94, **93, 94**

Rouse Simmons, 99–100

Scourge, 41–42

searching for, 108–109, 111

shallow areas as cause of, 90–91

sonar image of, **41, 110**

in Thunder Bay, Michigan,
86–88, **87**

shorelines, formation of, 10–11

slaves, 40

Sleeping Bear Dunes National
Lakeshore, 11

smallpox, 31

sonar, **41, 110,** 111

songs, 73–74

Soo Locks, 59, **59**

South Manitou Island Lighthouse,
Michigan, **80**

South Superior Entry Lighthouse,
81

Southport (Kenosha), Wisconsin,
44

Split Rock Lighthouse, Two Harbors, Minnesota, **79**

square-rigged vessels, 55, **56**

St. Lawrence Seaway, map of, **21**

steam, **4**

steamships
    Charles H. Bradley, **63**, **64**
    City of Racine, **63**, **64**
    City of Toledo, 78
    fire danger on, 95
    Montana, 95–96, **95**, **96**
    New Orleans, 90–92, **91**
    origins of, 60–61
    "palace steamers," **62**
    Pewabic, 93, **93**, **94**, **116**
    propeller steamers, 63, **63**
    and shipping cargo, 62
    Western World, **62**

swamps. *See* wetlands

T

Thunder Bay Island Lighthouse, Michigan, **82**

Thunder Bay, Michigan
    map of shipwrecks in, **87**
    New Orleans shipwreck in, 91–92, **91**
    Pewabic shipwreck in, 93–94, **93**, **94**
    as "shipwreck alley," 86
    shipwrecks in, 88

Thunder Bay National Marine Sanctuary and Underwater Preserve, 116–117

trading, between Europeans and Natives, 22

travel routes
    Erie Canal as, 46–48

Great Lakes as, 46
of Native people, 50
See also waterways

treaties, 50–51

tributaries, defined, 15

Tyrone, **67**

U

United States
    formation of, 34–35
    and War of 1812, 36–40

US Coast Guard, 75, **83**

US Lifesaving Service, 75

US Lighthouse Service, 75

V

Vega, **71**

voyageurs, 23–24, **23**

W

War of 1812
    African American sailors in, 40
    warships used in, 36–38, 41–42
    weapons used during, 39, **39**

wars
    French and Indian War, 33–34
    Revolutionary War, 34–35
    War of 1812, 36–39

warships
    during War of 1812, 37–38
    weapons on, 39, **39**

water
    different forms of, **4**
    drinking, in Great Lakes, 9

power of, 5
qualities of, 4

watersheds
    defined, 14
    map of Michigan and Wisconsin, **14**

waterways
    changes to, 52
    efficiency of, 54
    Erie Canal, 46–48
    of Great Lakes region, **11**
    to Michigan and Wisconsin (1800s), **54**
    as Native peoples' transportation routes, 16–17
    routes during fur trade, **29**

weapons
    long guns, **39**, **41**
    on warships, 39, **39**

weather, 89

Welland Canal, 58–60, 67

Western World, **62**

wetlands, 12–13, **13**

whalebacks, 66

Whitefish Bay, **83**

wild rice harvests, **17**

Williams, Jesse, 40

Wind Point Lighthouse, Racine, Wisconsin, **70**

Wisconsin
    as one of the Great Eight states, 48–50
    water routes to (1800s), **54**

Wisconsin Historical Society, 18, 108

Wisconsin Wetlands Association, 13

women, 73, 82